GRADE

MW00682195

# Presidents

School Specialty. Publishing

Columbus, Ohio

Send all inquiries to:
School Specialty Publishing
8720 Orion Place
Columbus, OH 43240-2111

ISBN 0-7696-5504-1

4 5 6 7 8 9 10 HPS 12 11 10 09

# George Washington *(1732-1799)*

George Washington
1st President
Party: Federalist
Term: 1789-1797

George Washington was born on a Virginia farm. He was given a primary education, then, as a young man, worked as a surveyor measuring land. When his half-brother died, Washington inherited his land and a home, Mount Vernon. Tall and strong, he liked outdoor work and the army. He became an officer in the Virginia militia and fought to push the French out of the upper Ohio River valley. In fighting at Fort Duquesne (now Pittsburgh, Pennsylvania), Washington learned Indian techniques and battle strategies.

By the end of the French and Indian War, Washington was a well-known officer. The Continental Congress asked him to become commander in chief of the Continental army in the Revolutionary War. Outnumbered by the enemy, the army never had enough supplies and were not as well trained as the British. Washington trained the army, gave them discipline, and kept up their hopes. Even in the winter of 1777-1778, when he and his men were nearly starving and freezing at Valley Forge, Washington refused to give up. His wife, Martha, joined him there and helped nurse sick soldiers. Training continued through the winter. In June 1778, the army followed Washington to a victory over the British in Monmouth, New Jersey. It was such determination, along with luck and good allies, that allowed Washington and his army to win the war.

After the Revolution, Washington tried to retire to Mount Vernon. But he was called back to become chairman of the Constitutional Convention—the gathering of delegates responsible for creating a fresh plan of government for the United States. When this plan, the Constitution, was approved, he was elected the first president of the United States and

served two terms. As president, Washington helped unite the new country. He listened to arguments from all sides, then steered a middle course. He was so well known for his strength and fairness that foreign countries were willing to accept and trade with the new nation. There is little wonder that Congress decided to name the new capital city in the District of Columbia after him.

*It is a myth that George Washington's false teeth were made out of wood. They were made from other teeth— those of humans and animals—and also from tusks!*

**Read the sentences about George Washington and his presidency.**
**Then complete the sentences by filling in each blank.**
**Use the word list if you need help.**

★ Washington fought for the British against the Indians and this country:

_____.

★ Washington's home colony, or state, was _____.

★ Washington was _____ of the Constitutional
Convention.

★ Alexander _____ served as Secretary of the
Treasury under Washington.

★ The Whiskey Rebellion was a result of farmers refusing to pay a federal

_____.

★ Washington served as a _____ during the
Revolutionary War.

★ Washington retired to his home, Mount _____,
after his presidency.

★ Washington worked to keep the nation _____,
or free from alliances that might result in war.

★ Thomas Jefferson was Washington's Secretary of

_____.

★ Washington married a young widow named _____.

━━━━━━━ *Word List* ━━━━━━━

| Chairman | general | neutral | Vernon |
|----------|---------|---------|---------|
| France | Hamilton | State | Virginia |
| | Martha | tax | |

# *John Adams* (1735-1826)

John Adams
2nd President
Party: Federalist
Term: 1797-1801

His enemies called him "His Rotundity" and laughed at his stuck-up manners. Yet John Adams worked hard all his life to shape and serve the nation he loved.

Adams grew up on a Massachusetts farm. He was educated at Harvard University and became a lawyer. As a young man, Adams took on the difficult task of defending the British soldiers who fired into a mob of colonists in the Boston Massacre. He entered the Massachusetts legislature and was caught up in the fight against Britain for colonial rights. Adams was an important member of the Continental Congress, and after urging Thomas Jefferson to write the first draft of the Declaration of Independence, Adams continued to play an important role in the making of that historic document. He spent several years in Europe, working as a diplomat for the new United States.

Because of his political career, Adams was often separated from his wife, Abigail. They wrote to each other frequently. "Remember the ladies," Abigail once wrote, "and be more generous and favorable to them than your ancestors!"

Soon after Adams returned from Europe, he was elected vice president under George Washington. He disliked the job much of the time because he had so little power. After eight years, though, he was in a position to be elected president.

The presidency proved to be hard for Adams. His toughest job was maintaining peace with France. He managed to do so, in part, by creating a navy that would threaten anyone planning to attack an American ship. However, keeping the peace did not help Adams's political career. Alexander Hamilton and other members of the Federalist Party had wanted to fight France. They withdrew their support for Adams and he lost the election in 1800.

John and Abigail Adams enjoyed a long retirement in Massachusetts. Adams' favorite activity was reading. "You will never be alone with a poet in your pocket," he declared. As a very old man, he was overjoyed when his son John Quincy Adams became president.

**Read the clues about John Adams and his presidency.**
**Then complete the puzzle using the word list on the next page.**

## ★ *Across* ★

3. First name of Adams's wife
4. Adams's biggest challenge was keeping the peace with this country.
6. Adams liked to keep the work of this kind of writer in his pocket.
7. Adams worked with Jefferson on the Declaration of _____.

8. Adams grew up on one in the countryside.
9. Adams served as a member of this government body in the Massachusetts colony.
11. As a lawyer, Adams defended the British soldiers involved in the Boston _____.

## Down

1. Adams's home colony or state
2. Adams's profession
4. Party that withdrew support for Adams after one term
5. Adams was the first president to live in the _____ House in Washington, D.C.
10. Number of years Adams served as vice president

*Adams was the first president to live in the White House.*

## Word List

| ABIGAIL | FEDERALIST | LAWYER | MASSACRE |
| EIGHT | FRANCE | LEGISLATURE | POET |
| FARM | INDEPENDENCE | MASSACHUSETTS | WHITE |

# Thomas Jefferson *(1743-1826)*

Thomas Jefferson was born on a prosperous plantation in Virginia. Jefferson's accomplishments—in and out of politics—are amazing! He mastered many languages and was an expert on plants and crops, music, fine food, and Indian artifacts. He was trained in the law. Jefferson designed his own home, called Monticello, and the buildings at the University of Virginia, which he also founded. He created money for the United States and invented the swivel chair, among other things.

**Thomas Jefferson
3rd President
Party: Democratic-Republican
Terms: 1801-1809**

At age twenty-six, Jefferson became a member of the colonial legislature of Virginia. Although he did not fight in the Revolutionary War, Jefferson was an important member of the Continental Congress. He was the chief author of the Declaration of Independence. After the war, he wrote a statute, or law, of religious freedom for Virginia. He was a U.S. ambassador, or minister, to France when the Constitution was written, but he returned to serve in the first cabinet as President Washington's secretary of state. After serving as John Adams's vice president, Jefferson was elected president.

Jefferson headed the new Democratic Republican Party, an earlier form of today's Democratic Party. Jefferson and his party thought that the national government should be small and not interfere in private affairs. As president, Jefferson spent little money and cut the budgets of the army and navy.

Although Jefferson thought the government should stay within the bounds set by the Constitution, he could not resist buying the Louisiana Territory from France for the bargain price of $15 million. With the Louisiana Purchase, Jefferson nearly doubled the size of the United States.

After eight years in office, Jefferson retired to Monticello. On July 4, 1826, the fiftieth anniversary of the Declaration of Independence, Jefferson (and his old colleague John Adams) died.

**Read the clues about Thomas Jefferson and his presidency.
Then complete the puzzle using the word list on the next page.**

## ★ *Across* ★

3. Jefferson founded the Democratic _____ Party.
5. Jefferson reduced spending for this fighting force.
8. Jefferson died _____ years after the Declaration of Independence was written.
9. President for whom Jefferson served as vice president
11. Jefferson made a good deal for the Louisiana _____.
12. Jefferson's home

## Down

1. Jefferson was chief author of the _____ of Independence.
2. Jefferson was a U.S. _____ in France when the Constitution was written.
4. Jefferson's family business
6. Jefferson invented a form of this for the nation.
7. Jefferson was trained in this field.
10. Jefferson wrote an important Virginia law to protect the religious kind of this.
13. Number of terms Jefferson served as president

## The Lewis and Clark Expedition

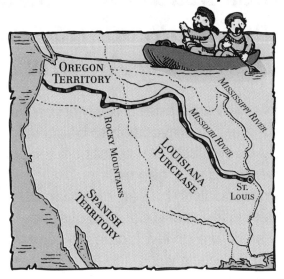

President Jefferson sent Meriwether Lewis and William Clark to explore the Louisiana Territory after its purchase.

## Word List

| | | | |
|---|---|---|---|
| ADAMS | FIFTY | MONEY | PURCHASE |
| AMBASSADOR | FREEDOM | MONTICELLO | REPUBLICAN |
| ARMY | LAW | PLANTATION | TWO |
| DECLARATION | | | |

# James Madison *(1751-1836)*, James Monroe *(1758-1831)*, and John Quincy Adams *(1767-1848)*

**James Madison**
**4th President**
**Party: Democratic-Republican**
**Terms: 1809-1817**

James Madison and James Monroe were the last leaders of the American Revolution to become presidents. John Quincy Adams, son of the nation's second president, represented a new generation.

James Madison helped create the U.S. Constitution. His notes on the secret debates over how to shape the U.S. government are an invaluable part of American history. In addition, Madison wrote the Bill of Rights, the first ten amendments to the Constitution.

Thomas Jefferson appointed Madison secretary of state (Monroe and John Quincy Adams later held the same job for different presidents). France and Britain were already at war, and the Democratic Republican Party wanted the nation to join France in the fight. After he was elected president, Madison declared war against Britain. In 1814, the British attacked Washington, D.C., burning the Executive Mansion (later called the White House) and other buildings, and forcing members of the government to flee for a time. In spite of the turmoil, Madison's life in Washington was a social success, thanks mostly to his wife, Dolley, who loved hosting parties. The War of 1812 ended in 1815 and inspired "The Star-Spangled Banner," a song that became the national anthem.

**James Monroe**
**5th President**
**Party: Democratic-Republican**
**Terms: 1817-1825**

James Monroe received some credit for postwar contentment. One newspaper nicknamed his time in office the "era of good feeling." During Monroe's administration, the United States acquired Florida from Spain. Spain and other European countries later threatened to retake their former colonies in Central and South America. Monroe issued the Monroe Doctrine, a document warning the countries of Europe not to create colonies in the Americas.

As a member of Monroe's cabinet, John Quincy Adams helped create the Monroe Doctrine and acquire Florida. However, Adams did not accomplish much during his time

**John Quincy Adams**
**6th President**
**Party: Democratic-Republican**
**Term: 1825-1829**

in office, because the majority of representatives in Congress were politically opposed to him. President Adams went swimming in the Potomac River every morning when the weather was good. He also kept an alligator as a pet! John Quincy Adams was not elected to a second term as president, but he did serve as a congressman after he left office. In that position, he worked against slavery and for people's rights and helped found the Smithsonian Institute in Washington, D.C.

**Words about James Madison, James Monroe, and John Quincy Adams and their presidencies have been scrambled. Rearrange the letters and write the correct word on each line. Use the word list if you need help.**

CERFAN

_____

TRMINDATIINOSA

_____

SERGNOCS

_____

ELODLY IMODNAS

_____

EROMNO RTCNEIDO

_____

NISAMOTSNIH

_____

ULOVTRINEO

_____

TGWSOHNIAN

_____

MPTOOCA

_____

RILDAFO

_____

TOSUTIOCINNT

_____

HITEW SHEOU

_____

## *Word List*

| | | | |
|---|---|---|---|
| ADMINISTRATION | DOLLEY MADISON | MONROE DOCTRINE | SMITHSONIAN |
| CONGRESS | FLORIDA | POTOMAC | WASHINGTON |
| CONSTITUTION | FRANCE | REVOLUTION | WHITE HOUSE |

# Andrew Jackson (1767-1845)

**Andrew Jackson**
**7th President**
**Party: Democratic**
**Terms: 1829-1837**

They called him "Old Hickory" because he was so tough. Andrew Jackson was born in a log cabin along the border of North and South Carolina and barely learned to read. At the age of thirteen, he became a messenger for the militia in the Revolutionary War and was captured by the British. When he refused to clean a British officer's boots, the man slashed Jackson's hand with a sword. The scar remained for life—and so did Jackson's fighting spirit. He fought Indians along the frontier and had become a general in the U.S. Army by the War of 1812. Old Hickory led American troops to victory over the British in the battle of New Orleans, and became famous for it nationwide. It did not seem to matter that the war had actually ended before the battle took place, as news of the peace had not arrived in time.

Jackson's supporters wanted him to be president after Monroe, but Jackson lost to John Quincy Adams when the close election had to be decided in the House of Representatives. Four years later, Jackson won. His wife, Rachel, died just before Jackson took office. His frontier followers showed up to celebrate his inauguration. The crowd muddied White House furniture, broke glasses, and overturned the punch. Refined Americans were horrified, but Jackson's friends called him the first "people's president."

In office, Jackson insisted he was there to represent the people, not to go along with Congress. He was the first president to veto many bills. He pushed for what he wanted, such as the removal of Indian tribes from the eastern United States in the 1830s. He also strengthened the hand of the federal government against the states. When South Carolina refused to obey a tariff law (a tax on imported goods), he was prepared to use force—until the state agreed to a compromise. After two terms, Jackson retired to Tennessee, as popular as when he was elected.

**Read the clues about Andrew Jackson and his presidency.**
**Then complete the puzzle using the word list on the next page.**

## Across

4. Jackson defeated the British at the battle of New _____.
5. Jackson fought in more than one of these.
6. Ceremony at the beginning of a presidency; Jackson's was riotous
9. Age at which Jackson served as messenger for the Revolutionary militia
11. Jackson forced Indian tribes from this part of the United States to move west of the Mississippi.
12. Jackson made officials in South _____ obey a federal tariff law.

14. Jackson was the first president to use this power often.

## Down

1. As a young man, Jackson fought these people.
2. Jackson was born in this kind of house.
3. Tax on imported goods, which South Carolina did not want to pay
7. Job Jackson had as a boy during the Revolutionary War
8. Rank Jackson attained in the U.S. Army
10. Uneducated, Jackson could barely do this.
13. First word in Jackson's nickname

*Jackson fought more than one duel during his lifetime.*

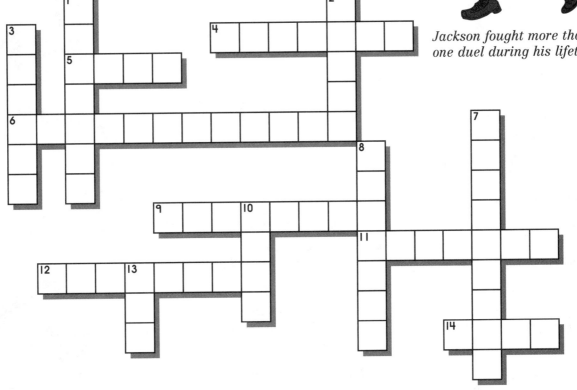

## Word List

| | | | |
|---|---|---|---|
| CABIN | EASTERN | MESSENGER | TARIFF |
| CAROLINA | GENERAL | OLD | THIRTEEN |
| DUEL | INAUGURATION | ORLEANS | VETO |
| | INDIANS | READ | |

# Martin Van Buren *(1782-1862)*, William H. Harrison *(1773-1841)*, and John Tyler *(1790-1862)*

Martin Van Buren was the first president to be born an American citizen (presidents before him were born British citizens), yet he spoke Dutch at home! That's because his family was part of the old Dutch settlement of Kinderhook, New York.

Van Buren was a good politician. He was able to "ride Andrew Jackson's coattails," rising from vice president during Jackson's second term to president in 1837. Van Buren's election campaign was the first in which rallies, sing-alongs, and slogans played an important role.

Van Buren ran into big trouble once he became president. The country was plunged into an economic depression. Too many people had borrowed money to buy land, expecting the value of land to rise. When it did not, they lost money. Banks and businesses closed, and many workers lost their jobs. Even though the depression was caused mostly by overspeculation and a natural economic downturn, it hurt the president's image. Van Buren was defeated after his first term by William Henry Harrison.

Harrison was an Ohio general, famous for winning the battle against Chief Tecumseh at the Tippecanoe River. Known as "Old Tippecanoe," Harrison ran for president with vice presidential candidate John Tyler. Harrison became ill while giving his inauguration speech in cold weather. It was the longest inauguration speech in American history—one hour and forty-five minutes! Afterward, Harrison said, "I am ill, very ill." He died one month after his inauguration.

Subsequently, John Tyler became president. Although Tyler was a Whig, as Harrison had been, he did not agree with most of the party's policies. The Whigs favored central government, while Tyler wanted the states to have more rights. He vetoed his own party's bills, including one that would create a national bank. However, just three days before he left office, Tyler did sign a bill to make Texas a part of the United States.

**Martin Van Buren**
**8th President**
**Party: Democratic**
**Term: 1837-1841**

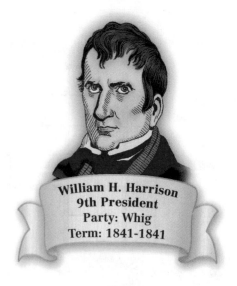

**William H. Harrison**
**9th President**
**Party: Whig**
**Term: 1841-1841**

**John Tyler**
**10th President**
**Party: Whig**
**Term: 1841-1845**

**Read the sentences about Martin Van Buren, William H. Harrison, and John Tyler and their presidencies. Then complete the sentences by filling in each blank. Use the word list if you need help.**

★ Van Buren was _____ in Andrew Jackson's administration.

★ _____ was the site of the battle from which Harrison got his nickname.

★ Harrison was president for one _____.

★ Van Buren spoke _____ at home.

★ After his inauguration, Harrison admitted he was

_____.

★ Tyler opposed the creation of a _____ bank.

★ The nation faced this economic problem while Van Buren was in office:

_____.

★ Snappy sayings, or _____, were an important part of Van Buren's campaign.

★ Van Buren lost for a second term because he could not improve the state of the

_____.

★ _____ was the Indian chief who was defeated by Harrison at Tippecanoe.

*Tyler introduced the polka to people at White House parties.*

## Word List

| | | | |
|---|---|---|---|
| **depression** | **economy** | **national** | **Tippecanoe** |
| **Dutch** | **ill** | **slogans** | **Vice President** |
| | **month** | **Tecumseh** | |

# James Polk (1795-1849), Zachary Taylor (1784-1850), and Millard Fillmore (1800-1874)

**James Polk**
**11th President**
**Party: Democratic**
**Term: 1845-1849**

James Polk was chosen by the Democrats partly because no one knew him well enough to be his enemy. He was the first dark-horse, or unlikely to win, presidential candidate. No alcohol was allowed in the White House during Polk's administration. He is said to have preferred water instead.

By the mid-1800's, American pioneers wanted to move west freely, but Mexico and Britain still claimed some of the land. Polk helped arrange an agreement with Britain to divide the Oregon Territory into two sections, one of which would become part of Canada. However, he could not pry California away from Mexico. In fact, the United States and Mexico were still disputing about the recently annexed Texas. Polk sent U.S. troops to Mexico, where they were attacked by Mexican forces. American troops easily defeated the Mexican army, and Polk arranged to pay Mexico for land that would one day become part of California, Nevada, Utah, Arizona, New Mexico, and Wyoming.

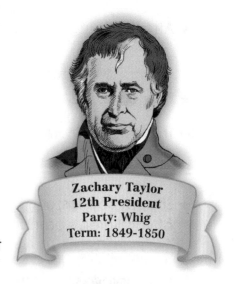

**Zachary Taylor**
**12th President**
**Party: Whig**
**Term: 1849-1850**

Polk retired after only one term and died soon after he left office. Polk's political rivals, the Whigs, nominated the army general whom Polk had sent to Mexico. His name was Zachary Taylor, also known as "Old Rough and Ready." Taylor did not have any political experience before entering office. Taylor brought his horse, Old Whitey, to the White House, where it grazed on the lawn. He focused on the major issue of the day—whether California and New Mexico would ban slavery when they entered the Union. The Southern states were afraid this would upset the balance of states and threatened to leave the Union. Taylor favored slavery, but he told Congress that he would lead an army against the Southern states if they tried to destroy the Union.

**Millard Fillmore**
**13th President**
**Party: Whig**
**Term: 1850-1853**

On July 4, 1850, President Taylor fell ill with stomach distress. He died five days later of cholera. Vice President Millard Fillmore, from New York, became president.

Fillmore was opposed to slavery, but he wanted to preserve the Union. He approved the Compromise of 1850, which had been proposed by Congress to relieve tensions between the North and the South. Among other things, the agreement allowed California to enter the Union as a free state, without slavery. It also set forth the Fugitive Slave Law, which required every state to allow the arrest and return of runaway slaves. Many Northerners were upset because this "compromise" seemed to favor slavery. Some Southerners were distressed that the federal government was now passing legislation on slavery rather than leaving it up to the states.

**Words about James Polk, Zachary Taylor, and Millard Fillmore and their presidencies have been scrambled. Rearrange the letters and write the correct word on each line. Use the word list if you need help.**

PISOMEMOCR

_____

AANDCA

_____

ONINU

_____

LVAEYSR

_____

SEWT

_____

WIGSH

_____

MICEOX

_____

RANELEG

_____

STAEMOCRD

_____

EREF

_____

RAYLOT

_____

RIFONALCIA

_____

## Word List

| | | | |
|---|---|---|---|
| CALIFORNIA | DEMOCRATS | MEXICO | UNION |
| CANADA | FREE | SLAVERY | WEST |
| COMPROMISE | GENERAL | TAYLOR | WHIGS |

# Franklin Pierce (1804-1869) and James Buchanan (1791-1868)

**Franklin Pierce**
**14th President**
**Party: Democratic**
**Term: 1853-1857**

Franklin Pierce, a handsome New Hampshire lawyer and politician, was not well known when he was elected president. If he seemed unhappy at times, people remembered that all three of his sons had died—the last one just before his inauguration.

As president, Pierce tried to get more land for the United States. He was unable to buy Cuba from Spain or take over Hawaii. However, in 1853, Pierce made the Gadsden Purchase, buying land from Mexico that today forms the Southern part of Arizona and New Mexico.

Pierce felt that each new state should decide for itself whether or not to have slavery. He signed the Kansas-Nebraska Act, overriding the 1820 Missouri Compromise, which outlawed slavery in the Northern part of the nation. When it became clear that the settlers in Kansas would decide whether or not to allow slavery in the new state, people on both sides of the issue rushed in. Violence resulted and the territory was nicknamed "Bleeding Kansas."

**James Buchanan**
**15th President**
**Party: Democratic**
**Term: 1857-1861**

The Democratic Party did not want to nominate Pierce again. They chose James Buchanan, who had not been involved in the Kansas-Nebraska Act or its violent aftermath. Buchanan was afraid the Southern states would leave the Union, so he tried to keep both sides satisfied. He supported the Supreme Court's decision in the Dred Scott case, which said that slaves and their descendents had no rights and suggested that the federal government could not stop any state or territory from having slavery. Many Americans were furious at the decision. Then Buchanan split his own party by asking Congress to accept Kansas as a slave state. Congress did not accept that plan, and Kansas remained a territory.

Buchanan is the only U.S. president who never married. His niece, Harriet Lane, acted as hostess while Buchanan was in the White House. Buchanan was not nominated by his party again. In 1860, Abraham Lincoln, of the antislavery Republican Party, was elected. In the last months of Buchanan's term, before Lincoln took office, states began to secede from the Union.

**Read the clues about Franklin Pierce and James Buchanan and their presidencies. Then complete the puzzle using the word list on the next page.**

## ★ Across ★

2. Lincoln belonged to this political party, which opposed slavery.

4. Buchanan asked Congress to accept Kansas as this kind of state.
6. Both Pierce and Buchanan belonged to this political party.
8. Pierce was the first president to celebrate this holiday with a tree in the White House.
9. Pierce's purchase of land in the Southwest was called the _____ Purchase.
10. People rushed into this territory to decide if it would be a free or slave state.
11. Buchanan sided with the decision in the Dred _____ case.

## Down

1. Land bought in the Gadsden Purchase became part of _____ Mexico.
3. Adjective used to describe the violent Kansas territory
4. Buchanan feared the Southern states would do this.
5. The Missouri Compromise of 1820 outlawed slavery in this area of the nation.
7. Adjective describing Pierce's looks
8. Island in the Caribbean that Pierce wanted to acquire.

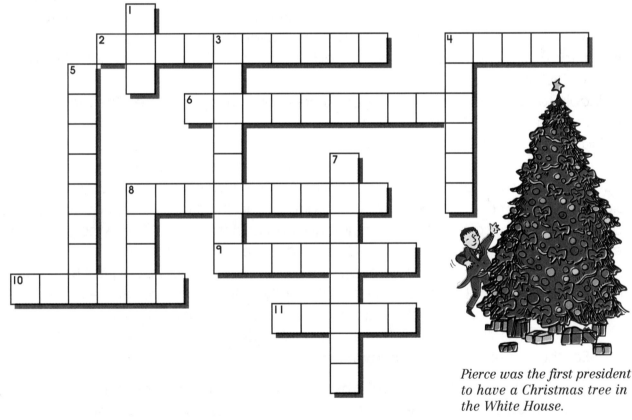

*Pierce was the first president to have a Christmas tree in the White House.*

## Word List

| | | | |
|---|---|---|---|
| **BLEEDING** | **GADSDEN** | **NEW** | **SCOTT** |
| **CHRISTMAS** | **HANDSOME** | **NORTHERN** | **SECEDE** |
| **CUBA** | **KANSAS** | **REPUBLICAN** | **SLAVE** |
| **DEMOCRATIC** | | | |

# Abraham Lincoln *(1809-1865)*

**Abraham Lincoln**
**16th President**
**Party: Republican**
**Term: 1861-1865**

Abraham Lincoln was born in a Kentucky log cabin and grew up on the frontier in Indiana and Illinois. Young Abe loved to read and often borrowed books that he read at night by firelight.

As a young man, Lincoln studied law on his own. He married Mary Todd, a woman some people believe had a bad temper, in 1842. He was elected to the Illinois state legislature, and then to the House of Representatives. He argued that slavery should not be allowed in new territories, although it was acceptable in the existing ones. When Lincoln ran for the U.S. Senate, he challenged his rival, Democrat Stephen A. Douglas, to a series of debates. Although he lost the election, the Lincoln-Douglas debates made Lincoln famous. People appreciated his homespun wit and wisdom. Two years later, he was elected president. Lincoln, and the antislavery Republican Party, wanted to preserve the Union, but the Southern states had already started to secede. Soon after Lincoln took office, Southerners fired on federal troops at Fort Sumter, South Carolina, and the Civil War began.

Lincoln faced enormous challenges as president during this time. The war became long and drawn out. On January 1, 1863, Lincoln issued the Emancipation Proclamation, freeing the slaves in the rebelling states. Lincoln worried greatly about the suffering of the nation's people during the war. During his famous Gettysburg Address in Pennsylvania, Lincoln asked Americans to continue fighting for freedom and democracy so that the soldiers would not have to die in vain. Lincoln walked the streets of the capital and the halls of the War Department late at night, grieving and thinking. After trying many other generals, Lincoln finally put Ulysses S. Grant in charge of the Union army.

Lincoln was reelected as the war drew to an end. He urged Congress to restore the nation as soon as rebel states promised their loyalty. "Blood cannot restore blood," he said, "and government should not act for revenge." Lincoln's plans for the future were cut short. He was shot at Ford's Theater in Washington, D.C., by John Wilkes Booth, a bitter Southerner seeking his own revenge.

**Read the clues about Abraham Lincoln and his presidency.**
**Then complete the puzzle using the word list on the next page.**

## ★ *Across* ★

1. Congressman Lincoln was known for opposing slavery in these places.
5. Last name of the person with whom Lincoln debated when he ran for Senate
8. Lincoln's _____ Proclamation declared an end to slavery in the Confederate states.

9. Kind of animal Jack, a pet in the Lincoln household, was
10. Lincoln's profession before he entered politics
11. The kind of city Washington, D.C., is; where Lincoln walked the streets worrying
12. Lincoln said, "Blood cannot restore ____."

## Down

1. Lincoln's wife's maiden name
2. Kind of building; where Lincoln was assassinated
3. Last state Lincoln lived in before he became president
4. The Lincoln-Douglas debates were part of a campaign for this kind of seat.
6. Lincoln tried out several of these before he settled on Grant.
7. Pennsylvania battleground where Lincoln gave a famous address

*Lincoln, shown here in his famous stovepipe hat, kept a pet turkey named Jack. The bird had been rescued from becoming a Thanksgiving dinner.*

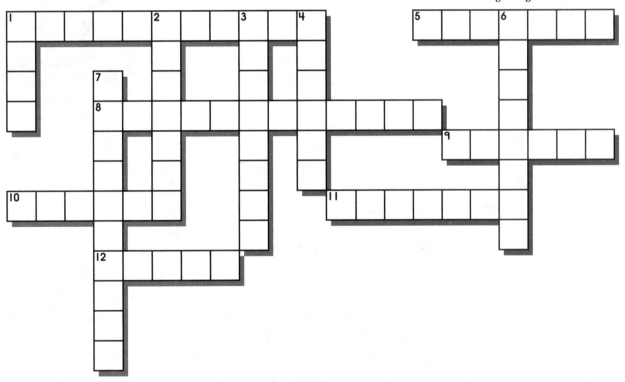

## Word List

| | | | |
|---|---|---|---|
| BLOOD | GENERALS | LAWYER | THEATER |
| CAPITAL | GETTYSBURG | SENATE | TODD |
| DOUGLAS | ILLINOIS | TERRITORIES | TURKEY |
| EMANCIPATION | | | |

# Andrew Johnson (1808-1875) and Ulysses S. Grant (1822-1885)

Andrew Johnson and Ulysses S. Grant, two very different presidents, oversaw the aftermath of the Civil War.

Johnson grew up without schooling in North Carolina. His sixteen-year-old bride helped him learn to write. A strong speaker, he took various governmental positions, from city council to the U.S. Senate. During the Civil War, he was the only Southerner who did not leave the Senate. He explained that he was against Lincoln, "but still I love my country." For Lincoln's second term, the Republican Party invited Johnson to run as his vice president, creating a "unity" ticket between the North and the South.

**Andrew Johnson**
**17th President**
**Party: Democratic**
**Term: 1865-1869**

As president, Johnson wanted to follow Lincoln's ideas for a lenient Reconstruction program, treating the former rebel states kindly while rebuilding after the war. Radical Republicans in Congress favored harsher treatment. They became angry after Johnson vetoed several of their bills, and they tried to get rid of him. He was impeached (formally accused of a crime) for dismissing his Secretary of War without the Senate's permission. The Senate tried Johnson and was one vote short of finding him guilty. Then, in 1867, the Republicans gained a two-thirds majority in Congress, which meant they could overturn Johnson's vetoes. Congress and the army took control of Reconstruction of the South.

**Ulysses S. Grant**
**18th President**
**Party: Republican**
**Terms: 1869-1877**

In the next presidential election, General Ulysses S. Grant, a hero of the Civil War, was elected. Grant, the son of Jesse and Hannah Simpson Grant, was originally named Hiram Ulysses, but his family called him Ulysses or 'Lyss. He decided to adopt the name Ulysses S. Grant after a clerical error was made listing his name as Ulysses Simpson at West Point. Grant was certainly at his best as general. Lincoln once said of him, "I can't spare this man. He fights." As president, though, Grant did not do as well. He had no political experience before taking office. Reconstruction of the South did not go smoothly. White Southerners resented Reconstruction, and secret groups such as the Ku Klux Klan terrorized African Americans. Although Grant was an honest man, his administration was marked by one scandal after another. Grant decided not to run for a third term.

**Read the clues about Andrew Johnson and Ulysses S. Grant and their presidencies. Then complete the puzzle using the word list on the next page.**

## Across

1. To formally accuse a president of a crime
4. Johnson was impeached (but not convicted) for dismissing the secretary of this department without Congress's permission.
7. Federal program intended to rebuild the South after the Civil War
10. Kind of book Grant wrote
11. Grant was popular as a war _____.
12. Johnson used this to stop the radical Republicans.

## Down

2. Johnson grew up in North _____.
3. Speech-maker; Johnson was a good one
4. Johnson's wife helped teach him to do this.
5. After impeachment charges were made, Johnson was tried by this group.
6. Grant's presidency was mired in these, which gave him a bad name.
8. Johnson was opposed to Lincoln but still had this for his country.
9. Kind of ticket created with Northerner Lincoln for president and Southerner Johnson for vice president

*Grant finished writing his memoirs a month before he died.*

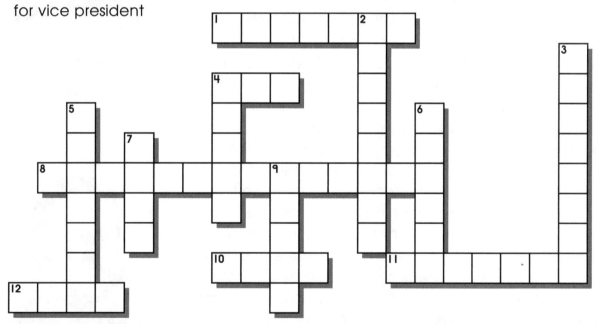

## Word List

| CAROLINA | MEMOIRS | SENATE | VETO |
| HERO | RECONSTRUCTION | SPEAKER | WAR |
| IMPEACH | SCANDALS | UNITY | WRITE |
| LOVE | | | |

# Rutherford B. Hayes *(1822-1893)*, James A. Garfield *(1831-1881)*, and Chester A. Arthur *(1829-1886)*

**Rutherford B. Hayes**
**19th President**
**Party: Republican**
**Term: 1877-1881**

Rutherford B. Hayes almost did not become president. He lost the vote of the electors (the representatives who elect the president) to Democratic candidate Samuel J. Tilden. However, the Republican Party challenged the voting results in three Southern states, as well as Oregon. The decision might have resulted in a deadlock if it had gone to Congress, which was made up of a Democratic House and a Republican Senate, but the Republicans and Democrats struck a deal. The questionable votes would go to Hayes, making him president, but he would have to pull the army troops out of the South and end Reconstruction. That is how Hayes became president. In the South, white Democrats took control and received little interference from the federal government for a long time.

Hayes entered the presidency with a solid reputation. He had been a Civil War general and governor of Ohio. Hayes and his wife, nicknamed, "Lemonade Lucy" because she banned alcohol in the White House, were religious and honest. Hayes made every effort to live by his motto: "He serves his party best who serves his country best."

**James A. Garfield**
**20th President**
**Party: Republican**
**Term: 1881-1881**

Like Hayes, James A. Garfield was a Republican from Ohio and an officer in the Civil War. He served seventeen years in Congress before he was elected president. Garfield was the first president to be fluent in Spanish. His vice president, Chester Arthur, was from a Republican group called the "Stalwarts." Garfield had been president for less than seven months when he was assassinated by a mentally disturbed man named Charles J. Guiteau, who cried, "I am a Stalwart; now Arthur is president!" Although it was later shown that Guiteau was not acting as part of a conspiracy for the Stalwarts, Chester Arthur entered the presidency with a cloud over his head. Some people thought the Stalwarts would stop at nothing to get what they wanted.

**Chester A. Arthur**
**21st President**
**Party: Republican**
**Term: 1881-1885**

Arthur was opposed to reform, but he did back a new civil service law, changing the way people got federal government jobs. He also improved the navy and the postal system. He had such a large wardrobe—including eighty pairs of pants!—that people called him "Elegant Arthur."

**Read the sentences about Rutherford B. Hayes, James A. Garfield, and Chester A. Arthur. Then complete the sentences by filling in each blank. Use the word list if you need help.**

★ The U.S. _____ system was improved by Arthur.

★ Hayes was a _____ in Ohio.

★ Garfield served seventeen years in _____ before he was elected president.

★ Garfield was fluent in _____.

★ Arthur improved this fighting force: the _____.

★ Arthur helped reform _____ jobs.

★ Garfield was killed in the seventh _____ of his presidency.

★ _____ are the representatives who elect the president.

★ The civil _____ is the system of government jobs.

★ Arthur had eighty pairs of _____.

--- *Word List* ---

| | | | |
|---|---|---|---|
| **Congress** | **government** | **Navy** | **service** |
| **Electors** | **governor** | **pants** | **Spanish** |
| | **month** | **postal** | |

# Grover Cleveland *(1837-1908)*

At the end of Grover Cleveland's first term, his wife told the White House servants to take care of things while she and her husband were gone. They'd be sure to return, she said, in four years! It turned out to be true—Grover Cleveland was the only president to serve a term, be out a term, and then serve a second term.

Cleveland was known as an honest reformer. He cleaned up government as Buffalo's mayor, then as governor of New York. In 1884, Cleveland ran for president as a Democrat, receiving extra support from a reform-minded group of Republicans called the "mugwumps."

**Grover Cleveland
22nd & 24th President
Party: Democratic
Terms: 1885-1889
1893-1897**

In office, Cleveland enforced the Pendleton Civil Service Act, which had been signed by President Arthur. Thousands of jobs once given out as political favors were made available to the public. Cleveland made the railroads give back land they had claimed illegally. He vetoed bills that would have given pensions to Civil War veterans who had not been wounded. Cleveland wanted a low tariff, but he was unable to achieve this.

In 1888, Cleveland ran for reelection against Benjamin Harrison. It was a tight race, but Cleveland lost. Four years later, Cleveland rode a large vote into office again, defeating Harrison this time. Soon afterward, the panic of 1893 led to a major economic depression. Cleveland tried to change the U.S. treasury system but was unable to improve the situation and received a lot of the blame for the country's economic troubles. Earlier, in 1892, Cleveland sent federal troops to end the Pullman railroad strike in Chicago. Although that move was favored by businesses, it angered union workers.

Although Cleveland was not always popular, his oldest daughter, Ruth, was so well liked that she had a candy bar named after her. Baby Ruth bars are still sold in stores today.

*An illustration of Cleveland's White House wedding to his much younger wife, Frances*

Use the word list to help you find the words about
Grover Cleveland and his presidency that are hidden in the block below.
Some of the words are hidden backward or diagonally.

```
A K H O D E P P R E S S I O N R
O M C G U R O S B H L P A U Y E
R T O A O J O B S A E J P O G E
T H W C P V S N C R I O E W N L
A Q K I R S E I M R S T N D J E
R U W H N M L R Q I D H S A R C
C G I C V R T X N S F F I R A T
O S Z L U E D B P O N I O Q O I
M D A E F T B M U N R S N P S O
E A R P Y O U G N Z F F S V C N
D O O E V W F H I L M M V S T E
G R Y B G T F K O X H E Y A K Y
C L A U I R A R N F T O M I J R
K I M Z P L L C B O U H R B U S
X A W R E F O R M E R T D H Q X
T R E A S U R Y S Y S T E M V N
```

## *Word List*

| | | | | |
|---|---|---|---|---|
| BUFFALO | GOVERNOR | PENSIONS | RUTH | TWO TERMS |
| CHICAGO | HARRISON | RAILROADS | STRIKE | UNION |
| DEMOCRAT | JOBS | REELECTION | TARIFF | VETO |
| DEPRESSION | MAYOR | REFORMER | TREASURY | |
| | MUGWUMPS | | SYSTEM | |

# Benjamin Harrison *(1833-1901)* and William McKinley *(1843-1901)*

**Benjamin Harrison**
**23rd President**
**Party: Republican**
**Term: 1889-1893**

Benjamin Harrison was an Indiana lawyer, an officer in the Civil War, and a senator. When he ran against Grover Cleveland for president, he got votes largely because his name was so well known. His grandfather, William Henry Harrison, had been president many years earlier. Harrison also had the backing of business leaders who wanted a high tariff, or tax, on imported goods. Harrison signed the McKinley Tariff Act, written by House member and future president William McKinley. The new tariff raised prices and increased profits for U.S. manufacturers. People with less money, such as farmers, laborers, and especially America's flood of new immigrants, were unhappy with the high prices. They also wanted better wages and working conditions. At the end of Harrison's term, President Cleveland was voted back in to office.

**William McKinley**
**25th President**
**Party: Republican**
**Term: 1897-1901**

Although McKinley supported a high tariff, he was voted into office because the economy had worsened during Cleveland's second term. McKinley had been a lawyer, a congressman, and governor of Ohio. As a presidential candidate, McKinley received support from the powerful business and financial leaders in the Republican Party, who feared his opponent, William Jennings Bryan, would upset the economy by changing the basis of U.S. money from gold to silver.

The Spanish-American War marked McKinley's first term. American newspapers published sensational stories about Cuba's fight for independence from Spain, urging the United States to help free Cuba. This "yellow journalism" was only partly true, but it convinced many people that the United States should act. After the United States became involved in the Spanish-American War, Cuba won its independence, and the United States gained control of the Philippines, Puerto Rico, and Guam. McKinley later accepted Hawaii as a U.S. territory and divided the Samoan Islands with Germany. Only seven months into his second term, McKinley was assassinated by Leon Czolgosz, an anarchist who was disturbed by social injustice.

Words about Benjamin Harrison and William McKinley and their presidencies have been scrambled. Rearrange the letters and write the correct word on each line. Use the word list if you need help.

CRANHASTI

_____

NOSERTA

_____

VERSLI

_____

ROGERVON

_____

FARIFT

_____

SCTRANFEMUAUR

_____

MAUG

_____

YREALW

_____

BACU

_____

AIHAIW

_____

CEMOONY

_____

CARBILUNEP

_____

*Harrison's nick-name was "Little Ben."*

## Word List

| | | | |
|---|---|---|---|
| **ANARCHIST** | **GOVERNOR** | **LAWYER** | **SENATOR** |
| **CUBA** | **GUAM** | **MANUFACTURERS** | **SILVER** |
| **ECONOMY** | **HAWAII** | **REPUBLICAN** | **TARIFF** |

# *Theodore Roosevelt* (1858-1919)

Theodore Roosevelt
26th President
Party: Republican
Term: 1901-1909

As a child, Theodore Roosevelt was so sick with asthma and other illnesses that he had to be tutored at home instead of going to school. When he was thirteen, he began an exercise program and eventually became strong and energetic. His enthusiasm for fresh air and exercise lasted the rest of his life.

Born well off, Roosevelt went to Harvard University, then held a number of government positions. He worked as a rancher in the Dakota Territory for two years after his mother and his first wife died. He worked in President McKinley's administration during the Spanish-American War before deciding to join the fight himself. After the war, Roosevelt was elected governor of New York.

Roosevelt became vice president during McKinley's second term. He was made president when McKinley was assassinated in 1901. Roosevelt was just forty-two years old at the time, making him the youngest president in U.S. history.

During his two terms as president, Roosevelt accomplished a lot. He believed people should have a fair, or "square," deal. He tried to break up large business groups that controlled prices, called "trusts." He also managed to raise wages for coal miners. He supported the Pure Food and Drug Act and the Meat Inspection Act, raising standards for food and medicine. He received the Nobel Peace Prize for his role as mediator in the Russo-Japanese War. He built up the navy and encouraged the building of the Panama Canal on the isthmus of Panama. Roosevelt said it was best to "speak softly and carry a big stick."

Roosevelt also supported the creation of many national parks and forests. Once, while on a hunting trip, Roosevelt refused to shoot a bear cub. A toy maker created the first "Teddy Bear" in honor of Roosevelt.

The White House was a lively place while Roosevelt was in office. He always made time to play with his six adventurous and fun-loving children.

**Read the clues about Theodore Roosevelt and his presidency.
Then complete the puzzle using the word list on the next page.**

## *Across*

3. Roosevelt worked for laws that would preserve the wilderness in national parks and _____.
4. Term for the kind of deal Roosevelt promised voters
7. Healthy activity that Roosevelt favored
9. Roosevelt fought in the _____-American War.

10. Some players of this game were members of the Rough Riders.
11. Narrow land between bodies of water; the Panama Canal was built across one
12. Territory where Roosevelt ranched for two years

## Down

1. Large business combinations that Roosevelt tried to break up
2. Roosevelt was elected to this position after the Spanish-American War.
5. Number of children Roosevelt had
6. Health problem Roosevelt experienced as a child
8. Roosevelt said, "Speak softly and carry a big _____."

*Roosevelt formed the Rough Riders, a cavalry regiment, with friends including cowboys from the west and polo players from the east.*

## Word List

| | | | |
|---|---|---|---|
| **ASTHMA** | **FORESTS** | **POLO** | **SQUARE** |
| **DAKOTA** | **GOVERNOR** | **SIX** | **STICK** |
| **EXERCISE** | **ISTHMUS** | **SPANISH** | **TRUSTS** |

# William H. Taft (1857-1930) and Woodrow Wilson (1856-1924)

**William H. Taft**
**27th President**
**Party: Republican**
**Term: 1909-1913**

William H. Taft grew up in Cincinnati, Ohio. He was an Ohio state court judge before he became governor of the Philippines, which were recently gained through the Spanish-American War. In 1904, he returned to the United States to become President Roosevelt's Secretary of War. Roosevelt wanted Taft to succeed him as president when he retired, and Taft easily won the election.

Soon after taking office, Taft found out that being president was difficult and often "lonesome." Many people, including Theodore Roosevelt, thought Taft acted too conservatively, but he did his best to carry out Roosevelt's policies. For example, Taft's administration attempted to break up ninety trusts, or business combinations. He supported the establishment of a federal income tax, which was charged according to the amount a person earned.

**Woodrow Wilson**
**28th President**
**Party: Democratic**
**Term: 1913-1921**

The Republicans nominated Taft for a second term. Roosevelt, unhappy with the job Taft was doing, decided to run for president again and formed his own political party. As a result, the Republican vote was split and the election went to the Democratic candidate, Woodrow Wilson.

Woodrow Wilson was one of the most learned presidents. He was a professor at and president of Princeton University before he was elected governor of New Jersey. Just two years later, he became president.

Wilson is most famous for his role as a leader in World War I. He named "Fourteen Points" he thought were needed to create a lasting peace once the war was over. The most important one was the formation of the League of Nations, where countries could meet to resolve disputes. The Treaty of Versailles contained some of the points Wilson had proposed, but he was forced to compromise on several issues.

At home, though, Wilson could not get the Senate to agree to the treaty. Wilson became ill during a trip to rally public support for the treaty. Soon afterward, he suffered a stroke and did not appear publicly for months. His wife, Edith, took messages to him and announced his decisions. Some historians believe that Edith may actually have been making the decisions herself. The treaty was never approved by Senate.

**Words about William Taft and Woodrow Wilson and their presidencies have been scrambled. Rearrange the letters and write the correct word on each line. Use the word list if you need help.**

EAPEC

_____

AETRYT

_____

TINCREONP

_____

LORVEOSET

_____

MESLNEOO

_____

IPPLPNHIEIS

_____

SOREPOSRF

_____

SUTSRT

_____

YECTASRRE

_____

NOTREEUF

_____

NETASE

_____

INCTCININA

_____

## Word List

| | | | |
|---|---|---|---|
| CINCINNATI | FOURTEEN | ROOSEVELT | SENATE |
| LONESOME | SECRETARY | PRINCETON | TREATY |
| TRUSTS | PEACE | PROFESSOR | PHILIPPINES |

# Warren G. Harding (1865-1923) and Calvin Coolidge (1872-1933)

**Warren G. Harding**
**29th President**
**Party: Republican**
**Term: 1921-1923**

Warren G. Harding and Calvin Coolidge, two very different men, took office as president and vice president in 1921. Harding was tall, handsome, and likeable, but he had spent most of his time as a senator doing favors for friends back home in Ohio. Coolidge was a strict, conservative New Englander. He became famous when, as a governor of Massachusetts, he broke up a Boston police strike by calling in the National Guard. "There is no right to strike against the public safety," he declared, "by anyone, anywhere, any time."

Harding probably won the presidency because he promised a return to "normalcy" after World War I. He was opposed to the League of Nations, but he called for the Washington Disarmament Conference. There, the United States and other nations agreed to reduce the size of their navies.

**Calvin Coolidge**
**30th President**
**Party: Republican**
**Term: 1923-1929**

Harding preferred gambling, drinking, and playing golf to work. He gave friends from Ohio jobs in Washington, D.C. Many of them were without ability; others were careless of their duties. The press called them the "Ohio Gang." Three years into his term, Harding died suddenly, probably from a heart attack. After Harding's death, many scandals became known publicly, including the Teapot Dome scandal in which the secretary of the interior was found guilty of accepting over $3 million in bribes to rent government land to oil drillers.

*Coolidge spoke so little he was called "Silent Cal."*

Calvin Coolidge was an honest president. He made government more efficient and economical. He did not believe government should interfere in private business, even though people seemed to be gambling on the stock market. "The business of America is business," he declared. Coolidge served the remainder of Harding's term plus one of his own. He retired a few months before the stock market crashed in 1929, leading to the worst economic depression in U.S. history.

**36**

Use the word list to help you find the words about Warren G. Harding
and Calvin Coolidge and their presidencies that are hidden in the
block below.  Some of the words are hidden backward or diagonally.

```
L E V I T A V R E S N O C D T R
A E P T E A P O T D O M E G E I
P L A N A T I O N A L G U A R D
S Y X G I D H T M O K T I G J B
N O S H U P R E K I R T S N O U
O H I O Y E P T C N E C P A M S
I C L S R C O O L I D G E G R I
S P E K H S Y F B U Z N Y O U N
S R N G O V E R N O R I V I M E
E E T G A B N X J A E W R H E S
R S E N A T O R G K T J F O U S
P I K I E M Z L I B R I B E S F
E D Q D N O R M A L C Y O D I Q
D E G R V T E G J F N P L N L U
A N M A S S A C H U S E T T S W
U T M H S T O C K M A R K E T B
```

## Word List

| | | | |
|---|---|---|---|
| BRIBES | GOVERNOR | NAVY | SENATOR |
| BUSINESS | HARDING | NORMALCY | SILENT |
| CONSERVATIVE | LEAGUE OF NATIONS | OHIO | STOCK MARKET |
| COOLIDGE | MASSACHUSETTS | OHIO GANG | STRIKE |
| DEPRESSION | NATIONAL GUARD | PRESIDENT | TEAPOT DOME |

# Herbert C. Hoover (1874-1964)

**Herbert C. Hoover
31st President
Party: Republican
Term: 1929-1933**

Herbert Hoover was perhaps most remarkable for all the things he did when he was not president. By profession, he was a mining engineer, educated in the first class at Stanford University in California. As a young man, he managed mines all over the world and became very wealthy. Hoover was living in London when World War I began, and he organized a committee to help his fellow Americans get home from Europe. Soon he was heading the Commission for Relief in Belgium, which helped distribute aid in war-torn Europe.

President Wilson took advantage of Hoover's experience, making him the wartime U.S. food administrator, responsible for getting Americans to save food so more would be available for the troops. Then, after World War I, Hoover headed a council to distribute food to the hungry in Europe.

By this time, Hoover was so well known that President Harding named him secretary of commerce. He did so much for the country that people called him "Undersecretary of Everything Else." Hoover was untouched by the scandals of Harding's administration.

In 1928, Hoover was elected president—his first elective office. Just seven months into his presidency, the Great Depression struck. About a quarter of all Americans were out of work; many were homeless and hungry. Hoover increased government loans to banks and businesses and supported some public works projects, but he did not think it was right for government to give aid to poor people or create jobs with borrowed money. He was afraid that would destroy the individual American's drive to succeed. Although he had not created the conditions that led to the economic troubles, Hoover was blamed for the depression. At the end of his term, he was defeated in a landslide.

Hoover continued to help others after he left office. In 1946, President Truman made Hoover chairman of the Famine Emergency Commission in Europe. He later worked on two different commissions to help make government more efficient.

**Read the clues about Herbert C. Hoover and his presidency.
Then complete the puzzle using the word list on the next page.**

## ★ *Across* ★

3. Hoover headed Belgium's Commission for _____.
4. Word used for camps of the poor and unemployed during the depression
5. Term for a big election win
6. Mass hunger; Hoover helped fight this in Europe
8. Hoover trained for this profession in college.

10. University Hoover attended

## Down

1. As secretary of commerce, Hoover was called "_____ of Everything Else."
2. The last commissions Hoover served on were supposed to make government more_____.
5. British city where Hoover lived for a time
7. As a young man, Hoover managed these.
9. Help; given out by many Hoover-led groups
11. Number of terms Hoover served

*The tent and shack cities of the unemployed during the Great Depression were called "Hoovervilles."*

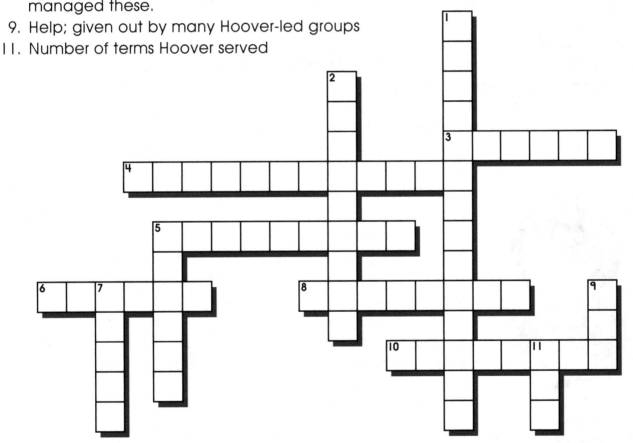

## Word List

| | | | |
|---|---|---|---|
| **AID** | **FAMINE** | **LONDON** | **RELIEF** |
| **EFFICIENT** | **HOOVERVILLES** | **MINES** | **STANFORD** |
| **ENGINEER** | **LANDSLIDE** | **ONE** | **UNDERSECRETARY** |

# Franklin D. Roosevelt *(1882-1945)*

**Franklin D. Roosevelt**
**32nd President**
**Party: Democratic**
**Terms: 1933-1945**

Franklin Delano Roosevelt, often called "FDR," was born into a wealthy and well-connected family. In fact, he was related to eleven former American presidents. He was also distantly related to the woman he married. Trained in the law, FDR served in the New York State Senate before President Wilson made him assistant secretary of the navy.

At age 39, FDR contracted polio, which left his legs paralyzed. For the rest of his life, he wore leg braces and used crutches or a wheelchair. He ran for governor of New York in 1928. When the Great Depression struck, he took measures to help suffering people in his state.

The Democrats nominated Roosevelt for president in 1932. He offered Americans the New Deal, promising that the government would do much more to relieve suffering and end the depression. In the so-called "First Hundred Days" of his presidency, FDR put through a storm of new laws. He temporarily closed banks to end panic withdrawals, then reopened them with federal help and deposit insurance. Later, he fought for laws that laid a foundation of security for Americans, creating Social Security, unemployment insurance, and federal aid to dependent children. FDR's radio talks, called "fireside chats," gave people new confidence. "The only thing we have to fear is fear itself," Roosevelt said.

FDR would have done even more to control business and industry, but the Supreme Court blocked some of his measures. In 1937, he tried to enlarge the size of the Court in order to appoint judges who would agree with him, but the plan failed.

The nation appreciated FDR's strong leadership during World War II. He died at the start of his last term in 1945. Roosevelt was elected to four terms—no other president had been elected to more than two terms! Congress later passed a law limiting presidents to two consecutive terms in office.

*Eleanor Roosevelt, one of the greatest first ladies, worked hard to achieve equality for people of all races and wrote the Universal Declaration of Human Rights.*

**40**

Use the word list to help you find the words about
Franklin D. Roosevelt and his presidency that are hidden in the block
below.  Some of the words are hidden backward or diagonally.

```
A M Y J O S Y R A T E R C E S L
P N J F E P O A N S M Z T M A G
A U N E M P L O Y M E N T W N D
R P L A M H A S J E L B Q R H D
E L E R L Y F W R M E E U F K G
P O L I O S D I O E A I H I U S
H E R T O G O V E R N O R R E P
P B A N K S C S L P O Y D E N I
H L T A Y L P F O U R I F S A C
L M L D X I L I P S G Q D I V R
E N K E R A U G E C A L N D Y U
L U P R E J W Z D X L O R E R T
E M I D T Y T I R U C E S F A C
V L W N L S E R R I F G V I Z H
E E T U W A V R D N G D K O N B
N W G H H U M A N Y E N R A C E
```

## Word List

| | | | |
|---|---|---|---|
| BANKS | FEAR | HUNDRED | RACE |
| CRUTCH | FIRESIDE | LAW | SECRETARY |
| ELEANOR | FOUR | NAVY | SECURITY |
| ELEVEN | GOVERNOR | NEW DEAL | SUPREME |
| FDR | HUMAN | POLIO | UNEMPLOYMENT |

# Harry S. Truman (1884-1972)merriemm

**Harry S. Truman**
**33rd President**
**Party: Democratic**
**Terms: 1945-1953**

Harry S. Truman had served only eighty-two days as vice president when Franklin Roosevelt's death pushed him into the presidency. As a young man, Truman was not able to afford to go to college, but he had read every book in the Independence, Missouri, library by the time he was fifteen. He entered politics as a county official, then was elected senator. Roosevelt chose Truman to be his running mate for 1944 because his last vice president was seen to be too liberal.

Truman proved to be an energetic president who did not hesitate to attack his critics. In his first term, Truman tried to pass new civil rights laws and expand Social Security, but Congress refused to cooperate. Truman's greatest challenges came from abroad, however. World War II came to an end in Europe soon after he took office, but the war continued in the Pacific. Truman decided to use the newly developed atomic bomb on the Japanese. It is estimated that more than 130,000 people were killed in the atomic explosions at Hiroshima and Nagasaki. Historians still argue over whether or not the bombing was needed to end the war and therefore save lives that might have been lost in an invasion of Japan.

At the end of the war, Truman put through the Marshall Plan, a vast aid program for Europe. He also came to Berlin's aid when the Soviets threatened to take control of it in 1948. With roads closed, he ordered planes to carry supplies to the parts of the city that were controlled by the United States and its allies. The airlift succeeded, and the Soviets opened the city again.

*Bess "The Boss" Truman.*

During his second term, Truman focused much of his attention on the Korean War. In 1950, communist North Korea invaded South Korea. Truman sent troops to Korea, then asked for backing from the United Nations, an international organization that had been formed in 1945. Truman was very concerned about stopping the spread of communism.

Truman's wife and daughter were so much a part of his life that White House staff called them "the Three Musketeers." His wife, Bess, often gave him valued advice, and Truman called her "the Boss."

**42**

Words about Harry S. Truman and his presidency have
been scrambled. Rearrange the letters and write the correct
word on each line. Use the word list if you need help.

FILATIR

_____

MOICTA

_____

ICOSLA CUTRYESI

_____

ETESMSKURE

_____

MARHHOISI

_____

LIBNER

_____

DNINEPEECNDE

_____

MUSMCOMIN

_____

HLARAMSL APLN

_____

TINDEU SITONNA

_____

TENASOR

_____

EKAOR

_____

## Word List

| AIRLIFT | COMMUNISM | KOREA | SENATOR |
| ATOMIC | HIROSHIMA | MARSHALL PLAN | SOCIAL SECURITY |
| BERLIN | INDEPENDENCE | MUSKETEERS | UNITED NATIONS |

# Dwight D. Eisenhower (1890-1969)

Dwight D. Eisenhower
34th President
Party: Republican
Terms: 1953-1961

"I like Ike!" was Dwight D. Eisenhower's campaign slogan, and it was what people said about him all his life.

Eisenhower grew up in Abilene, Kansas. He attended West Point military academy and became a career officer. At the beginning of World War II, he was asked to command the War Plans Division of the War Department. His global strategy and early plan for the invasion of France were so good that President Roosevelt put him in charge of the U.S. Army in Europe. Soon he was heading the Allied forces there, coordinating armies and officers from six different countries. By the end of the war, Eisenhower, who had many good ideas and got along well with people, was an international hero. Both political parties wanted him to be their presidential candidate, but he didn't commit until 1952, when he decided to run as a Republican.

Eisenhower declared that he had already taken part in war and, as president, wanted to make peace. After his inauguration, Eisenhower helped arrange a peace agreement between North and South Korea, ending the Korean War. Like Truman, Eisenhower worried about communism spreading to more countries. He put forth the Eisenhower Doctrine, which said that any country in the Middle East threatened by communists could ask for U.S. aid. He sent troops to Lebanon when they were requested. Eisenhower also tried to deal directly with Soviet communist leaders in summit talks, although these stopped for a time when an American U-2 spy plane was shot down over the Soviet Union.

At home, in a time of prosperity, Eisenhower did little to change the policies set by Presidents Roosevelt and Truman. He enforced existing civil rights laws, sending federal troops to make sure African American students could attend school in Little Rock, Arkansas, in 1957. He helped initiate the interstate highway system. And Eisenhower warned the nation that American arms-makers were combining with the armed forces in a "military-industrial complex" that was dangerous and expensive for the nation.

**Read the clues about Dwight D. Eisenhower and his presidency.
Then complete the puzzle using the word list on the next page.**

## ★ Across ★

1. Eisenhower's nickname
4. Eisenhower worried about the spread of this political belief system.
7. Eisenhower's hometown
9. Eisenhower said that, as president, he wanted to make _____.
10. Eisenhower renamed the presidential retreat _____ David after his grandson.

11. The Eisenhower _____ said Middle East countries threatened by communism could get U.S. aid.

## Down

1. Kind of highway system Eisenhower helped start
2. Eisenhower met with leaders of the Soviet Union in this kind of meeting.
3. Continent where Eisenhower served as chief of the armed forces
5. Both political parties wanted Eisenhower to be their _____ after the war.
6. Asian country where Eisenhower helped to make peace
8. Eisenhower sent troops to this Middle Eastern country.
9. Second word in the name of the military academy Eisenhower attended
10. Eisenhower sent federal troops to Little Rock to enforce _____ rights laws.

*Eisenhower painting at Camp David, the presidential retreat formerly called "Shangri-La," which he renamed for his grandson David*

## Word List

| ABILENE | CIVIL | IKE | PEACE |
|---|---|---|---|
| CAMP | COMMUNISM | INTERSTATE | POINT |
| CANDIDATE | DOCTRINE | KOREA | SUMMIT |
|  | EUROPE | LEBANON |  |

# John F. Kennedy *(1917-1963)*

John F. Kennedy started life with many advantages. He was good looking and wealthy. In fact, he was the first president since George Washington to turn down his salary (he donated it to charities instead). He was also from a large, close family. His brothers and sisters helped him throughout his political career. And Kennedy was a talented thinker and writer. His book, *Profiles in Courage*, about courageous senators in history, won a Pulitzer Prize in 1957.

**John F. Kennedy
35th President
Party: Democratic
Term: 1961-1963**

Jack, as he was known to friends and family, went to Harvard, served in the navy during World War II, and became a congressman and then a senator for his home state of Massachusetts. Finally, in 1960, Kennedy was able to achieve his most important goal—the presidency. Kennedy's strong speaking ability helped him win the first televised debates between presidential candidates.

As president, Kennedy started the Peace Corps, which sent American volunteers to serve in poor or underdeveloped countries. His Alliance for Progress was meant to strengthen ties and trade among the nations of the Americas.

In 1961, Kennedy supported an attack on communist Cuba. The Bay of Pigs invasion was an embarrassing failure. The next year, however, Cuba was the scene of a Kennedy policy triumph. Aerial pictures showed that the Soviets were placing missiles in Cuba. President Kennedy told the Soviets to remove the missiles or risk war. After one tense week, Soviet leader Nikita Khrushchev withdrew the missiles. In 1963, tensions eased a little when Kennedy signed a treaty with Britain, France, and the Soviet Union to stop nuclear testing in the atmosphere, underwater, and in outer space.

At home, Kennedy favored strong civil rights laws and worked hard for desegregation in schools. However, it is hard to know what more Kennedy might have accomplished; he was assassinated after only a few years in office. On November 22, 1963, Kennedy was shot during a parade in Dallas, Texas. The alleged assassin, Lee Harvey Oswald, was killed soon afterward, so the public may never know exactly why or how Kennedy was assassinated.

*The years Kennedy spent in the White House with Jackie, Caroline, and John Jr. were compared to King Arthur's Camelot, a time of great happiness that was cut short by tragedy.*

Words about John F. Kennedy and his presidency have
been scrambled.  Rearrange the letters and write the correct
word on each line.  Use the word list if you need help.

MASGCNRONSE

_____

VRKHSCHEHU

_____

THACSEMASTSUS

_____

DRAHRVA

_____

YBA FO GPIS

_____

BESEATD

_____

ITREGNSEEDOAG

_____

SALADL

_____

AMELTOC

_____

LASWOD

_____

CEPAE PORSC

_____

TILUPRZE

_____

## Word List

| BAY OF PIGS | DALLAS | HARVARD | OSWALD |
| CAMELOT | DEBATES | KHRUSHCHEV | PEACE CORPS |
| CONGRESSMAN | DESEGREGATION | MASSACHUSETTS | PULITZER |

# Lyndon B. Johnson *(1908-1973)*

Lyndon B. Johnson grew up in Johnson City, a small town named after his grandfather. Johnson's father and both his grandfathers had served in the Texas state legislature. Maybe that is why, when Lyndon was born, his father rode a horse around town shouting that a future U.S. senator had just come into the world.

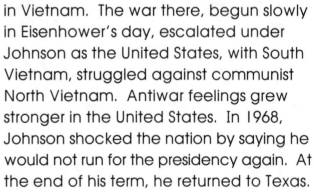

**Lyndon B. Johnson
36th President
Party: Democratic
Terms: 1963-1969**

Johnson taught high school briefly before he entered the House of Representatives and then the Senate. By 1955, he was majority leader (leader of the Democrats) in the Senate. Johnson tried to get his party's presidential nomination in 1960 but agreed to run as vice president when Kennedy was chosen. Johnson became president when Kennedy was assassinated and was easily elected in his own right in 1964.

As Americans mourned Kennedy, Johnson got certain laws through Congress that Kennedy had wanted. He managed to pass several major civil rights laws, including ones protecting the right of African Americans to vote and forbidding employers from discriminating against people on the basis of race or sex. Johnson also got Congress to pass laws to improve housing, provide Medicare for elderly people without health insurance, and protect the environment. He was aiming, he said, for a "Great Society" in which all people would be able to take part and prosper.

However, Johnson's dreams were thwarted. The new civil rights laws did not bring equality and jobs to all poor inner city African Americans. Frustrations increased and some cities were torn apart by riots. Meanwhile, young men were being drafted to fight

in Vietnam. The war there, begun slowly in Eisenhower's day, escalated under Johnson as the United States, with South Vietnam, struggled against communist North Vietnam. Antiwar feelings grew stronger in the United States. In 1968, Johnson shocked the nation by saying he would not run for the presidency again. At the end of his term, he returned to Texas.

*Johnson and his family all had similar names: Lyndon Baines, Lady Bird, Lynda Bird, and Luci Baines.*

Use the word list to help you find the words about
Lyndon B. Johnson and his presidency that are hidden in the block below.
Some of the words are hidden backward or diagonally.

```
K E N N E D Y L P R S I E D L C
L G R A N D F A T H E R S Y N I
N R E A B A F D O D W E R M B V
S E Y A C R M Y A R N C O A N I
Y A C O P E R B D I S W H N E L
E T T N N C Y I A O L L O T S R
H S N M A J O R I T Y X O E H I
H O U S I N G D U S C V R I T G
D C E T P M N O V E P T I V L H
T I Y C Z O L U D E M O C R A T
M E N V I R O N M E N T B U E S
L T O W S E L G R A R P D S H I
I Y R A B E S E N A T O R L A T
B R X I O T A U S W Z R L A L S
R E C Y J S S E R G N O C M N T
T A H L N C L M U M A B Y T I C
```

## Word List

| | | | |
|---|---|---|---|
| CITY | GRANDFATHERS | JOBS | RIOTS |
| CIVIL RIGHTS | GREAT SOCIETY | KENNEDY | SENATOR |
| CONGRESS | HEALTH | LADY BIRD | TEXAS |
| DEMOCRAT | HORSE | MAJORITY | VIETNAM |
| ENVIRONMENT | HOUSING | RACE | VOTE |

# Richard M. Nixon (1913-1994)

"I am not a crook," Richard M. Nixon insisted when people accused him of lying. But it turned out that he was guilty of one of the worst presidential scandals in history, known as "Watergate."

Nixon's accomplishments before Watergate form a long list. As a young senator from California, he was picked to be Dwight Eisenhower's vice president. In that position, Nixon traveled the world on diplomatic missions. He lost a close presidential election to John F. Kennedy, then lost another election for California governor. He told the press that they wouldn't "have Nixon to kick around any more," but Nixon never gave up easily. Within six years, he had been elected president.

**Richard M. Nixon**
**37th President**
**Party: Republican**
**Term: 1969-1974**

President Nixon's first priority was ending the war in Vietnam. He began a program, which he called "Vietnamization" of the war. American soldiers were slowly brought home as the bombing of North Vietnam was intensified and South Vietnamese soldiers were given training. Finally, Nixon got a cease-fire agreement signed with North Vietnam and pulled the last Americans out of the region. However, the North and South continued to fight until 1975, when the North won.

Nixon helped arrange a cease-fire between Israel and its Arab neighbors, Egypt and Syria. He was the first president to visit communist China. Back home, he tackled rising prices with federal wage and price controls—a daring move.

In 1972, Nixon was easily reelected, but during the campaign five agents of CREEP, the Committee to Re-Elect the President, were caught burglarizing the Democratic National Committee headquarters at the Watergate apartment complex in Washington, D.C. Nixon claimed he knew nothing about the theft of important records, but the scandal grew as the Senate Watergate Committee took evidence in televised hearings. The turning point came when the Supreme Court ordered Nixon to turn over tape recordings he had made. The tapes proved he had lied and covered up illegal actions. Nixon resigned on August 9, 1974. He was pardoned by the new president, Gerald Ford, soon afterward.

**Read the clues about Richard M. Nixon and his presidency.
Then complete the puzzle using the word list on the next page.**

## Across

2. Last name of president who pardoned Nixon
6. Acronym (initials) for the Committee to Re-Elect the President
7. Nixon's term for turning over the war to Vietnam
9. Part of Vietnam that won the war

10. Nixon staff members stole records from this political party.
11. Kind of missions Nixon made abroad for Eisenhower
13. Nixon helped arrange a cease-fire between Israel and Syria and _____.

## Down

1. Nixon was the first president to visit this communist country.
3. Nixon decided to do this when evidence showed he was guilty.
4. Nixon's home state
5. Term used for the Nixon scandal
6. Nixon daringly placed these on wages and prices to keep them down.
8. Court that ordered Nixon to turn in his tapes
12. Nixon said, "I am not a _____."

*Nixon gave a famous speech in which he denied taking gifts in return for favors, and stated that he was going to keep Checkers, a dog he had been given.*

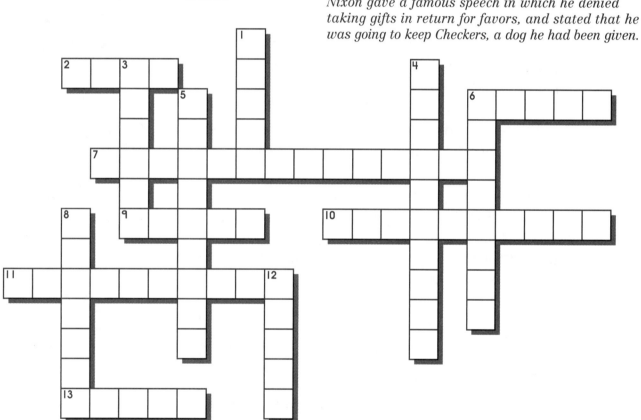

## Word List

| | | | |
|---|---|---|---|
| CALIFORNIA | CREEP | EGYPT | SUPREME |
| CHINA | CROOK | FORD | VIETNAMIZATION |
| CONTROLS | DEMOCRATIC | NORTH | WATERGATE |
| | DIPLOMATIC | RESIGN | |

# Gerald R. Ford *(1913-2006)* and James (Jimmy) E. Carter, Jr. *(1924- )*

**Gerald R. Ford**
**38th President**
**Party: Republican**
**Term: 1974-1977**

Gerald R. Ford of Michigan was minority leader (leader of the Republicans) in the House of Representatives when Richard Nixon asked him to replace Spiro Agnew as vice president. Agnew had resigned after being accused of income tax cheating and accepting bribes. Nixon wanted a man with a reputation for honesty, and he got one. The Senate and the House approved Nixon's choice, as is called for in the Twenty-fifth Amendment to the Constitution.

When Nixon resigned because of the Watergate scandal, Ford became president. Ford was the first person to take this office without ever having been elected president or vice president. Soon after he became president, Ford gave Nixon a full pardon, absolving him of any crimes he may have committed. This move angered many people and damaged Ford's chances in the next presidential election.

In 1976, newcomer Jimmy Carter was elected. James Earl Carter, who preferred to be called Jimmy from childhood on, sold peanuts while growing up in Plains, Georgia. Carter had been governor of Georgia for one term but had no national government experience. Carter had high ideals and a relaxed, personable leadership style. He supported human rights around the world and pushed for environmental protection and arms control.

**James (Jimmy) E. Carter, Jr.**
**39th President**
**Party: Democratic**
**Term: 1977-1981**

Carter's greatest success in foreign policy was the signing of the 1979 Camp David Accords, which brought peace between Israel and Egypt. He also arranged for Panama to receive control of the Panama Canal in 1999. Just before the last year of Carter's presidency, Americans at the U.S. embassy in Tehran were taken hostage by a group of Iranian revolutionaries. The hostages were not released until the day Carter left office. The prolonged hostage crisis, along with a limping economy, caused Carter to lose his bid for a second term.

*James Earl Carter; a country boy, was known as Jimmy from childhood on.*

Jimmy Carter has continued to do diplomatic work since retiring from office. He has helped supervise free elections around the world and worked to provide housing for the poor in the United States.

**Words about Gerald R. Ford and Jimmy Carter and their presidencies have been scrambled. Rearrange the letters and write the correct word on each line. Use the word list if you need help.**

NAODRP

_____

SNUOGHI

_____

STEPNUA

_____

AERGGIO

_____

NAHMU STIGRH

_____

YLPCIO

_____

WEANG

_____

IARELS

_____

ROGNOREV

_____

MAAPNA

_____

ATGSEOSH

_____

DEEAMNNTM

_____

## Word List

| | | | |
|---|---|---|---|
| AGNEW | GOVERNOR | HUMAN RIGHTS | PARDON |
| AMENDMENT | HOSTAGES | ISRAEL | PEANUTS |
| GEORGIA | HOUSING | PANAMA | POLICY |

# Ronald Reagan (1911-2004)

Ronald Reagan
40th President
Party: Republican
Terms: 1981-1989

Ronald Reagan grew up in Illinois. While working as a radio sportscaster in Iowa, Reagan traveled to California. There, he took a Hollywood screen test and soon began making movies. He became a famous actor, working in films for nearly twenty-eight years. During the 1950's, he worked as a spokesman for General Electric, hosting a television show and giving speeches.

California Republicans noticed Reagan and asked him to run for governor. During his two terms as governor, Reagan cut down the number of people on welfare. He criticized university students who were protesting and cut funds for higher education.

Reagan was elected president in 1980, winning such popularity with his speeches that the press called him "the Great Communicator." He cut taxes while increasing defense spending, which led to a record-high national debt. He urged Congress to support anticommunist movements in Nicaragua, Angola, and elsewhere around the world. In 1983, he sent U.S. troops to overthrow the government of the tiny island of Grenada. Although Reagan built up arms, he also met with Soviet leader Gorbachev in a series of summit meetings, easing relations with the Soviet Union.

Scandal struck Reagan's administration when it was revealed that U.S. officials had sold arms to Iranian kidnappers in exchange for American hostages being held in Lebanon. In addition, profits from the arms sales had gone to the Nicaraguan "contras," a group of people who were rebelling against their government, in spite of Congress's decision not to support the contras. Reagan had pledged never to negotiate with terrorists. Reagan claimed he had nothing to do with the Iran-contra affair, but many people on his staff were involved.

At the end of Reagan's second term, the economy was strong. Despite the earlier scandal, Reagan left office as one of the most popular presidents of the century. A few years later, Reagan announced that he had been diagnosed with Alzheimer's disease, an incurable illness that leads to loss of memory.

**Read the clues about Ronald Reagan and his presidency.**
**Then complete the puzzle using the word list on the next page.**

## Across

1. Last name of Reagan's press secretary, paralyzed by shots aimed at the president
4. This improved in the second half of Reagan's presidency.
6. Reagan held summit meetings with this Soviet leader.
9. Reagan once gave speeches for _____ Electric.

10. Reagan's favorite candy
13. The contras were in this country.
14. While governor of California, Reagan spoke against this group of people.

## Down

2. Money owed; Reagan increased this for the nation
3. Alzheimer's disease causes loss of this.
5. Reagan was called "the Great _____."
7. In California, Reagan cut down on this aid to the needy.
8. Reagan increased spending on this.
11. The Iran-contra affair centered on profits gained from selling these.
12. Term for a rebel fighting against the Nicaraguan government

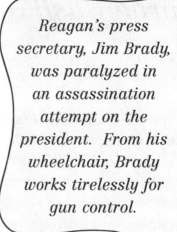

*Reagan's press secretary, Jim Brady, was paralyzed in an assassination attempt on the president. From his wheelchair, Brady works tirelessly for gun control.*

*Jelly beans were a favorite Reagan snack in the White House.*

## Word List

| | | | |
|---|---|---|---|
| **ARMS** | **CONTRA** | **GENERAL** | **NICARAGUA** |
| **BRADY** | **DEBT** | **GORBACHEV** | **STUDENTS** |
| **COMMUNICATOR** | **DEFENSE** | **JELLY BEANS** | **WELFARE** |
| | **ECONOMY** | **MEMORY** | |

# George Bush (1924- )

"Read my lips: no new taxes!" That's what George Bush promised when he was running for president. He was a Republican through and through, and he thought government should do less, not more.

Bush grew up in a wealthy Connecticut family. After a stint as a navy pilot during World War II and studying law at Yale University, he moved to Texas to enter the booming oil business. He made a small fortune there and was elected to the House of Representatives. Presidents Nixon and Ford gave him a series of important jobs: ambassador to the United Nations, chair of the Republican National Committee, chief of the U.S. Liaison Office in China, and director of the Central Intelligence Agency. Then, in 1981, he became Ronald Reagan's vice president. After two terms, he was easily elected as Reagan's successor to the presidency.

As president, Bush had to deal with a Democratic Congress. He signed a budget bill that reduced the amount the government had to borrow, but the bill also increased taxes, contrary to Bush's promise. The president had better luck in foreign affairs. The old Soviet Union was crumbling, a change that some people said was due to the triumph of American-style free enterprise. In the Persian Gulf, Iraqi leader Saddam Hussein tried to take over the tiny, oil-rich nation of Kuwait. Bush organized allies and sent troops to turn him back. The war was over quickly, with few lives lost.

The popularity Bush enjoyed at the end of the Gulf War faded as the economy drooped. Bush did not have any workable solutions to the problem of high unemployment. He lost the next election, leaving office after only one term.

**George Bush
41st President
Party: Republican
Terms: 1989-1993**

Barbara Bush marked her years as First Lady with a strong commitment to literacy.

Millie, the White House dog, is credited with writing a popular book actually written by her owner, Barbara Bush.

**Words about George Bush and his presidency
have been scrambled. Rearrange the letters and write the correct
word on each line. Use the word list if you need help.**

SPIL

_____

LOI

_____

SETXA

_____

LEAY

_____

AROMBADSSA

_____

RAABBAR

_____

TOLPI

_____

NURPLICAEB

_____

TUIWKA

_____

TUOLNNPYEEMM

_____

STAXE

_____

MOOCNYE

_____

## Word List

| AMBASSADOR | KUWAIT | PILOT | TEXAS |
| BARBARA | LIPS | REPUBLICAN | UNEMPLOYMENT |
| ECONOMY | OIL | TAXES | YALE |

# William Jefferson Clinton (1946- )

William Jefferson Clinton
42nd President
Party: Democratic
Terms: 1993-2001

William Jefferson Clinton, often called Bill, spent most of his childhood in Hot Springs, Arkansas, where he did well in school and learned to play the saxophone for fun. Clinton graduated from Georgetown University, attended Oxford University as a Rhodes scholar, and received a degree from Yale Law School before returning to Arkansas. There, he taught law and won his first election, as state attorney general. He then became governor on and off for several terms before he ran for president as a Democrat.

Clinton won the presidential election partly because he favored a center path between traditional Republican and Democratic ideas. In his first term, Clinton pushed for NAFTA—the North American Free Trade Agreement—which linked Mexico, Canada, and the United States, allowing companies and products to move freely across borders. Many Republicans favored this agreement, while some traditional Democrats did not.

Bill Clinton's health-care reform program did not pass through Congress. Clinton was criticized for placing his wife, Hillary, in charge of the effort. In 1996, Clinton signed an important welfare reform bill, which required people on welfare to seek work. And by the middle of his second term, there was a federal surplus—the first in a generation.

In foreign affairs, Clinton's attention turned to the former Yugoslavia, where ethnic groups clashed. In 1995, following a peace agreement, Clinton sent U.S. troops to Bosnia to keep the peace. Later, Serbs attacked ethnic Albanians in the neighboring province of Kosovo. This time, Clinton argued for a bombing campaign to stop Serb leader Slovodan Milosevic. The bombing succeeded, but many lives were lost. Clinton also played an important part in the Middle East peace agreement made between Israel and the Palestinians in 1993.

Clinton, no stranger to scandal, may be best remembered as the second president to be impeached, or formally accused of a crime. He was charged with lying under oath about his inappropriate relationship with a White House aide, Monica Lewinsky. At the Senate trial, Clinton was found not guilty of "high crimes and misdemeanors," in the language of the Constitution. Clinton apologized to the nation and returned to his job.

**Read the clues about Bill Clinton and his presidency. Then complete the puzzle using the word list on the next page.**

*Hillary Clinton became the first woman senator from New York. In 2008, she was a candidate for the Democratic nomination in the presidential election.*

## Across

1. First name of Clinton's wife

3. Clinton served in this position just before he became president.
6. Clinton was found not guilty of "high crimes and _____."
7. Last name of Serb leader who tried to take over Kosovo
8. Clinton's formal first name
9. Clinton had hoped to reform the way people pay for this type of care.
10. Province where the United States and its allies stopped a Serb takeover

## Down

2. Major conflicts occurred in Bosnia and Kosovo, located within this former country.
4. Initials for the North American Free Trade Agreement
5. Clinton taught this in Arkansas.
6. Clinton hosted the _____ East peace agreement between Israel and the Palestinians.
7. First name of White House aide involved in scandal with Clinton
8. Under Clinton's law, people who get welfare money must now seek this.

## Word List

| | | | |
|---|---|---|---|
| **GOVERNOR** | **LAW** | **MISDEMEANORS** | **WILLIAM** |
| **HEALTH** | **MIDDLE** | **MONICA** | **WORK** |
| **HILLARY** | **MILOSEVIC** | **NAFTA** | **YUGOSLAVIA** |
| **KOSOVO** | | | |

# George W. Bush (1946- )

George W. Bush
43rd President
Party: Republican
Term: 2001-2009

George Walker Bush was born on July 6, 1946 in New Haven, Connecticut. He spent most of his childhood in Texas, where his father, George Herbert Walker Bush became involved in the oil business. Bush graduated from Yale University and received his M.B.A. at Harvard University. He also served as an airman in the Texas Air National Guard.

Bush's father campaigned for president in the 1988 election. The young Bush assisted his father with the campaign, and his father won the election. After the election, George W. Bush and his wife, Laura, and daughters, Jenna and Barbara, settled in Dallas, Texas. Bush also worked in the oil business and was a managing general partner of the Texas Rangers baseball team.

After an unsuccessful run for congress in the late 1970's, Bush returned to politics and became governor of Texas in 1994. He was re-elected as governor in 1998 by a wide margin. He received national attention because of his policies, which included large tax cuts, educational reforms, and increased school funding. Even though Bush was criticized for not focusing more on racial issues, poverty, and environmental issues, he was already being touted as a possible presidential candidate.

Bush won the nomination for the Republican party's presidential candidate in 1999. He ran against Democratic candidate, Vice President Al Gore. The election of 2000 was one of the closest races in U.S. history. The outcome took weeks to determine—the winner of Florida was in dispute. The vote was extremely close in Florida, and election officials demanded a machine recount. When the machine recount declared Bush to have more votes, Gore asked for a manual recount. Finally, five weeks after the election, the U.S. Supreme Court put an end to the recounts. Although Gore won the popular vote, Bush received Florida's electoral votes and became the 43rd president.

Bush began his presidential career by focusing on tax cuts, education reform, and issues that he had concentrated on during his campaign. But, on September 11, 2001, Bush and the American nation turned their attention to a far more critical situation. Four commercial airliners were hijacked by terrorists and were intentionally crashed into the World Trade Center Towers, the Pentagon, and a field in Pennsylvania. Thousands of people were killed in the worst terrorist attack in United States history. Less than a month later, the U.S. began military strikes against Afghanistan, the country believed to be home to terrorist parties responsible for the attacks. In March 2003, the United States declared war on Iraq.

By the end of Bush's second term, the war in Iraq had become very unpopular. Some people still believed that America should stay in Iraq and finish what was started. Many others thought that it was time to bring American troops home. The war became a major topic in the next election.

**Use the word list to help you find the words about George W. Bush and his presidency that are hidden in the block below. Some of the words are hidden backward or diagonally.**

```
L I O G W A L K E R O G D R T M
A O N C N A C I L B U P E R B A
R E H T A F O L M R C T T A A K
L A R O T C E L E T Z C D R S S
T A R E P U I N O C L R S N E T
C A N E G L N P A O A H A N B N
E C F N A J O C F U T D C J A U
L J J P C R I G G R R S Y P L O
E A P B E D T L H T O S A W L C
X V E K R S A R A C N R D X S E
B L I J N N C W N D R L G H E R
P H H F O M U A I B E A W E S T
B E A I R E D W S A V M R S M B
S L T D S R E H T T O O K U D X
D A F L O R I D A F G S T M A J
N Y F L O Y R P N A S K D T H L
```

## Word List

| AFGHANISTAN | FATHER | LAURA | REPUBLICAN |
|---|---|---|---|
| BASEBALL | FIVE | MBA | TAX |
| COURT | FLORIDA | NATIONAL GUARD | TEXAS |
| EDUCATION | GORE | OIL | WALKER |
| ELECTORAL | GOVERNOR | RECOUNT | YALE |

# Barack Obama *(1961- )*

Barack H. Obama
44th President
Party: Democratic
Term: 2009-

In November of 2008, Barack Obama made history when he was elected the first African-American president of the United States. With his messages of unity and change, Obama was able to overcome barriers minorities had faced for hundreds of years.

Barack Obama was born in Hawaii in 1961. He was the child of an African father from Kenya and a white mother from Kansas. His parents divorced when he was two, and Obama was raised in Indonesia and Hawaii by his single mother and her parents.

In 1983, Obama graduated from Columbia University with a degree in political science. Instead of going straight to law school, he moved to Chicago. He worked there as a community organizer to improve the lives of the poor.

A few years later, Obama began law school at Harvard University. There, he became the first African-American president of a journal called the *Harvard Law Review*. He graduated with honors in 1991.

Obama returned to Chicago to teach law and work as a civil-rights lawyer. At work, Obama met a woman named Michelle Robinson. He didn't know it then, but she would one day become his greatest supporter. The couple married in 1992, and today they have two daughters: Malia and Sasha.

In 1996, Obama entered the world of politics. First, he served in the Illinois State Senate for eight years. Then, in 2004, he was elected to the U.S. Senate. He was only the third black senator to have ever been elected.

In February of 2007, Obama announced that he was running for president. The other likely nominee for the Democratic Party was Hillary Clinton—a senator and the wife of former president Bill Clinton. Either a woman or a black man would be on the 2008 ticket for the Democratic Party. New doors were opened for two groups of citizens—women and African Americans—who had had the right to vote for less than 100 years.

After a close contest with Clinton, Obama received the Democratic nomination. The next step was to begin the race for the White House. Obama and his running mate, Senator Joseph Biden, campaigned against Republicans John McCain and Sarah Palin. On November 4, Americans cast their votes and elected the next president: Barack Obama.

Obama ran a campaign based on change. Many Americans believed that the Iraq war was a mistake, and Obama vowed to bring American troops home. He also promised to look for energy sources other than expensive foreign oil. He made quality healthcare for all citizens a priority. Most important of all, he promised to unite Americans—across party lines, regardless of race, gender, or social class.

Words about Barack Obama and his presidency
have been scrambled. Rearrange the letters and write the correct
word on each line. Use the word list if you need help.

LCIMEEHL

_____

EHCGAN

_____

AESTNE

_____

OHGCIAC

_____

AIHWIA

_____

CRALHEHTEA

_____

RWLYAE

_____

RAEDOCMT

_____

EIBDN

_____

ARDVHRA

_____

IYUTN

_____

INFRAAC

_____

## Word List

| MICHELLE | UNITY | BIDEN | AFRICAN |
| HARVARD | SENATE | LAWYER | CHANGE |
| HAWAII | DEMOCRAT | CHICAGO | HEALTHCARE |

# Presidential Time Line

Write the names of these early nineteenth century presidents on the lines below each picture. Then, put them in the correct order by numbering the pictures from 1 to 4.

\#  ★  ___          \#  ★  ___          \#  ★  ___          \#  ★  ___

_____   _____   _____   _____

1800          1825          1850          1875          1900

19TH CENTURY

Write the names of these late nineteenth century presidents on the lines below each picture. Then, put them in the correct order by numbering the pictures from 1 to 4.

\#  ★  ___          \#  ★  ___          \#  ★  ___          \#  ★  ___

_____   _____   _____   _____

1800          1825          1850          1875          1900

19TH CENTURY

# Presidential Time Line

Write the names of these early twentieth century presidents on the lines below each picture. Then, put them in the correct order by numbering the pictures from 1 to 4.

\# ★ ___  \# ★ ___  \# ★ ___  \# ★ ___

_____   _____   _____   _____

1900        1925        1950        1975        2000

20TH/21ST CENTURY

Write the names of these late twentieth century/early twenty-first century presidents on the lines below each picture. Then, put them in the correct order by numbering the pictures from 1 to 4.

\# ★ ___  \# ★ ___  \# ★ ___  \# ★ ___

_____   _____   _____   _____

1900      1925      1950      1975      2000      2025

20TH/21ST CENTURY

# Presidential Compare and Contrast

Write the name of each president under his picture.

_____  _____      _____  _____

19TH CENTURY          1900              1950              2000

1800          1850          1900       20TH CENTURY

Name the presidents pictured above that match these statements. You may need to research some of the statements to write the name of the correct president.

We were born in Ohio. _____

I served as governor of a state. _____

Our vice presidents became presidents after us. _____

_____

The three of us were in office on the first day of a new century. _____

_____

I was born in the eighteenth century but died in the nineteenth. _____

I was born in the nineteenth century but died in the twentieth. _____

We were both assassinated while in office. _____

_____

We both have the same first name. _____

# Presidential Compare and Contrast

Write the name of each president under his picture.

_____    _____        _____        _____

19TH CENTURY                    1900            1950            2000

1800                1850                1900        20TH CENTURY

Name the presidents pictured above that match these statements. You may need to research some of the statements to write the name of the correct president.

⭐ We were both born in New York. _____

⭐ The two of us served as governors of states. _____

_____

⭐ We both served as vice president. _____

⭐ The three of us were in office during times of economic trouble. _____

_____

⭐ The three of us served only one term each. _____

_____

⭐ We were both elected as Republicans. _____

_____

⭐ We were both elected as Democrats. _____

# Presidents and Wars

Write the name of each president under his picture. Then, draw a line to the name of the war with which he is most closely associated. You may need to research the wars in order to match each war to the correct president.

19TH CENTURY
1800    1850    1900

1900    1950    2000
20TH CENTURY

_____

_____

_____

Revolutionary War
War of 1812
Civil War
Spanish-American War
World War I
World War II
Vietnam War
Persian Gulf War

_____

_____

_____

_____

_____

# Who's Who

Write the name of each president under his picture. Then, draw a line to another name by which each president was known. You may need to research the presidents in more detail to match each name to the correct president.

19TH CENTURY

1800     1850     1900

1900     1950     2000

20TH CENTURY

_____     _____     _____

Old Rough and Ready
Old Buck
Hero of Appomattox
Old Hickory
Little Magician
Ike
FDR
William Jefferson Blythe III

_____     _____     _____

_____     _____     _____

# Slogans and Quotations

Write the name of each president under his picture. Then, draw a line to the slogan or quotation with which he is associated. You may need to research the presidents in more detail to match each slogan or quotation to the correct president.

_____          _____          _____

"He serves his party best who serves his country best."

"First in war, first in peace, first in the hearts of his countrymen."

"Remember the Maine."

"Ask not what your country can do for you..."

"A house divided against itself cannot stand."

"... the world must be made safe for democracy."

_____          _____          _____

# Presidents and Important Events

Write the name of each president under his picture.  Then, draw a line to match each president with an important event with which he is associated.  You may need to research the events in order to match each event to the correct president.

19TH CENTURY
1800        1850        1900

1900        1950        2000        2050
20TH/21ST CENTURY

_____        _____        _____

The end of slavery
The end of Reconstruction
The end of the Cold War
The end of World War II
The Watergate scandal
The War in Iraq
The Lewis and Clark Expedition
The founding of the League of Nations

_____        _____

_____        _____        _____

# Presidents and Programs

Write the name of each president under his picture. Then, draw a line to match each president with an important program with which he is associated. You may need to research the programs in order to match each program to the correct president.

19TH CENTURY      1900      1950      2000

1800      1850      1900      20TH CENTURY

_____    _____    _____

14 Points

The New Deal

The Fair Deal

The Great Society

The Time of Good Feelings

The Full Dinner Pail

_____    _____    _____

★ Washington fought for the British against the Indians and this country:

**France**_____.

★ Washington's home colony, or state, was _____**Virginia**_____.

★ Washington was _____**Chairman**_____ of the Constitutional Convention.

★ Alexander _____**Hamilton**_____ served as Secretary of the Treasury under Washington.

★ The Whiskey Rebellion was a result of farmers refusing to pay a federal

**tax**_____.

★ Washington served as a _____**general**_____ during the Revolutionary War.

★ Washington retired to his home, Mount _____**Vernon**_____, after his presidency.

★ Washington worked to keep the nation _____**neutral**_____, or free from alliances that might result in war.

★ Thomas Jefferson was Washington's Secretary of

**State**_____.

★ Washington married a young widow named _____**Martha**_____.

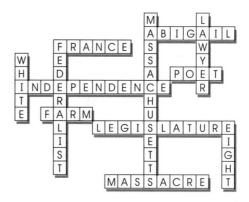

**7**

**9**

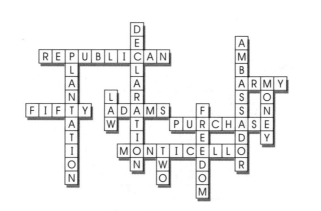

**11**

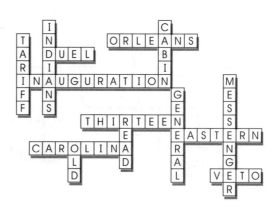

| | |
|---|---|
| CERFAN | ULOVTRINEO |
| **FRANCE** | **REVOLUTION** |
| TRMINDATIINOSA | TGWSOHNIAN |
| **ADMINISTRATION** | **WASHINGTON** |
| SERGNOCS | MPTOOCA |
| **CONGRESS** | **POTOMAC** |
| ELODLY IMODNAS | RILDAFO |
| **DOLLEY MADISON** | **FLORIDA** |
| EROMNO RTCNEIDO | TOSUTIOCINNT |
| **MONROE DOCTRINE** | **CONSTITUTION** |
| NISAMOTSNIH | HITEW SHEOU |
| **SMITHSONIAN** | **WHITE HOUSE** |

**13**

**15**

★ Van Buren was **Vice President** in Andrew Jackson's administration.

★ **Tippecanoe** was the site of the battle from which Harrison got his nickname.

★ Harrison was president for one **month**.

★ Van Buren spoke **Dutch** at home.

★ After his inauguration, Harrison admitted he was **ill**.

★ Tyler opposed the creation of a **national** bank.

★ The nation faced this economic problem while Van Buren was in office: **depression**.

★ Snappy sayings, or **slogans**, were an important part of Van Buren's campaign.

★ Van Buren lost for a second term because he could not improve the state of the **economy**.

★ **Tecumseh** was the Indian chief who was defeated by Harrison at Tippecanoe.

PISOMEMOCR
**COMPROMISE**

MICEOX
**MEXICO**

AANDCA
**CANADA**

RANELEG
**GENERAL**

ONINU
**UNION**

STAEMOCRD
**DEMOCRATS**

LVAEYSR
**SLAVERY**

EREF
**FREE**

SEWT
**WEST**

RAYLOT
**TAYLOR**

WIGSH
**WHIGS**

RIFONALCIA
**CALIFORNIA**

**17**

**19**

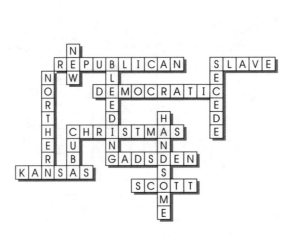

**21**

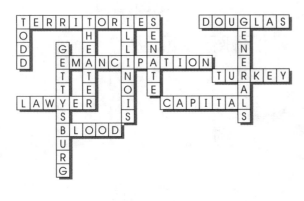

**23**

**25**

- ★ The U.S. **postal** system was improved by Arthur.
- ★ Hayes was a **governor** in Ohio.
- ★ Garfield served seventeen years in **Congress** before he was elected president.
- ★ Garfield was fluent in **Spanish**.
- ★ Arthur improved this fighting force: the **Navy**.
- ★ Arthur helped reform **government** jobs.
- ★ Garfield was killed in the seventh **month** of his presidency.
- ★ **Electors** are the representatives who elect the president.
- ★ The civil **service** is the system of government jobs.
- ★ Arthur had eighty pairs of **pants**.

**27**

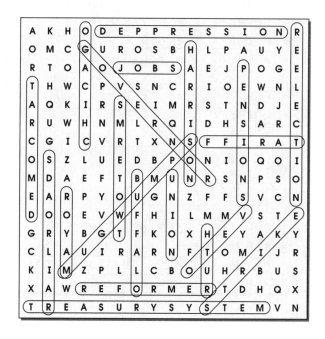

**29**

CRANHASTI
**ANARCHIST**

NOSERTA
**SENATOR**

VERSLI
**SILVER**

ROGERVON
**GOVERNOR**

FARIFT
**TARIFF**

SCTRANFEMUAUR
**MANUFACTURERS**

MAUG
**GUAM**

YREALW
**LAWYER**

BACU
**CUBA**

AIHAIW
**HAWAII**

CEMOONY
**ECONOMY**

CARBILUNEP
**REPUBLICAN**

**31**

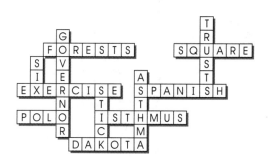

**33**

EAPEC
**PEACE**

AETRYT
**TREATY**

TINCREONP
**PRINCETON**

LORVEOSET
**ROOSEVELT**

MESLNEOO
**LONESOME**

IPPLPNHIEIS
**PHILIPPINES**

SOREPOSRF
**PROFESSOR**

SUTSRT
**TRUSTS**

YECTASRRE
**SECRETARY**

NOTREEUF
**FOURTEEN**

NETASE
**SENATE**

INCTCININA
**CINCINNATI**

**35**

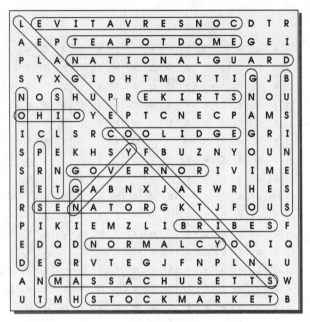

**37**

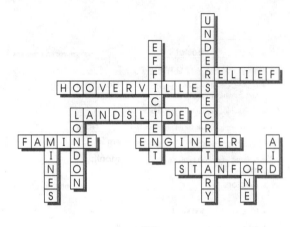

**39**

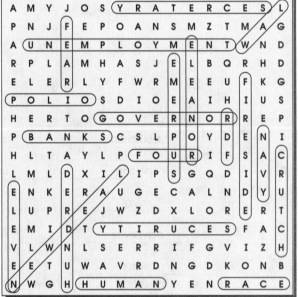

**41**

FILATIR
**AIRLIFT**

MOICTA
**ATOMIC**

ICOSLA CUTRYESI
**SOCIAL SECURITY**

ETESMSKURE
**MUSKETEERS**

MARHHOISI
**HIROSHIMA**

LIBNER
**BERLIN**

DNINEPEECNDE
**INDEPENDENCE**

MUSMCOMIN
**COMMUNISM**

HLARAMSL APLN
**MARSHALL PLAN**

TINDEU SITONNA
**UNITED NATIONS**

TENASOR
**SENATOR**

EKAOR
**KOREA**

**43**

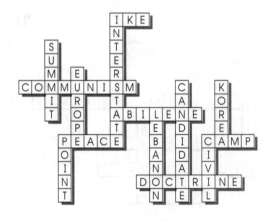

**45**

MASGCNRONSE
**CONGRESSMAN**

VRKHSCHEHU
**KHRUSHCHEV**

THACSEMASTSUS
**MASSACHUSETTS**

DRAHRVA
**HARVARD**

YBA FO GPIS
**BAY OF PIGS**

BESEATD
**DEBATES**

ITREGNSEEDOAG
**DESEGREGATION**

SALADL
**DALLAS**

AMELTOC
**CAMELOT**

LASWOD
**OSWALD**

CEPAE PORSC
**PEACE CORPS**

TILUPRZE
**PULITZER**

**47**

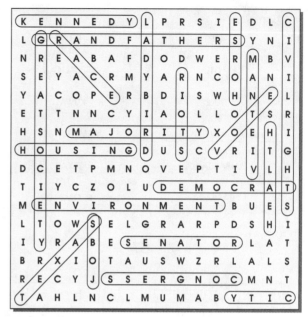

**49**

**51**

NAODRP
**PARDON**

SNUOGHI
**HOUSING**

STEPNUA
**PEANUTS**

AERGGIO
**GEORGIA**

NAHMU STIGRH
**HUMAN RIGHTS**

YLPCIO
**POLICY**

WEANG
**AGNEW**

IARELS
**ISRAEL**

ROGNOREV
**GOVERNOR**

MAAPNA
**PANAMA**

ATGSEOSH
**HOSTAGES**

DEEAMNNTM
**AMENDMENT**

**53**

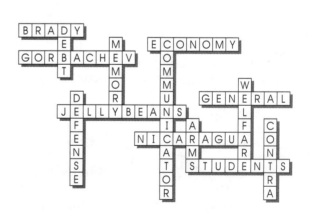

**55**

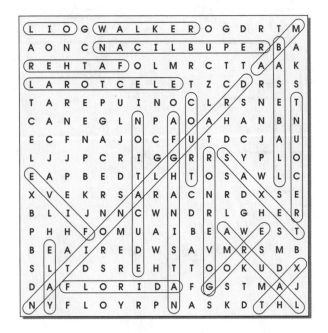

**57**

| | |
|---|---|
| SPIL | TOLPI |
| **LIPS** | **PILOT** |
| LOI | NURPLICAEB |
| **OIL** | **REPUBLICAN** |
| SETXA | TUIWKA |
| **TAXES** | **KUWAIT** |
| LEAY | TUOLNNPYEEMM |
| **YALE** | **UNEMPLOYMENT** |
| AROMBADSSA | STAXE |
| **AMBASSADOR** | **TEXAS** |
| RAABBAR | MOOCNYE |
| **BARBARA** | **ECONOMY** |

**59**

**61**

**63**

| | |
|---|---|
| LCIMEEHL | RWLYAE |
| **MICHELLE** | **LAWYER** |
| EHCGAN | RAEDOCMT |
| **CHANGE** | **DEMOCRAT** |
| AESTNE | EIBDN |
| **SENATE** | **BIDEN** |
| OHGCIAC | ARDVHRA |
| **CHICAGO** | **HARVARD** |
| AIHWIA | IYUTN |
| **HAWAII** | **UNITY** |
| CRALHEHTEA | INFRAAC |
| **HEALTHCARE** | **AFRICAN** |

4 Zachary Taylor   3 Andrew Jackson   1 Thomas Jefferson   2 James Monroe

2 Ulysses S. Grant   1 Abraham Lincoln   4 William McKinley   3 Grover Cleveland

**64**

*Presidents:Grade 4*     **78**     ©2008 School Specialty Publishing

| | | | |
|---|---|---|---|
| I | 4 | 2 | 3 |
| Theodore Roosevelt | Franklin D. Roosevelt | Woodrow Wilson | Herbert C. Hoover |

| | | | |
|---|---|---|---|
| 4 | 2 | I | 3 |
| Barack Obama | Richard Nixon | John F. Kennedy | William (Bill) Clinton |

65

| | | | |
|---|---|---|---|
| John Adams | James A. Garfield | William McKinley | William (Bill) Clinton |

Name the presidents pictured above that match these statements. You may need to research some of the statements to write the name of the correct president.

We were born in Ohio. **James A. Garfield and William McKinley**

I served as governor of a state. **William (Bill) Clinton**

Our vice presidents became presidents after us. **John Adams, James A. Garfield, and William McKinley**

The three of us were in office on the first day of a new century. **John Adams, William McKinley, and William (Bill) Clinton**

I was born in the eighteenth century but died in the nineteenth. **John Adams**

I was born in the nineteenth century but died in the twentieth. **William McKinley**

We were both assassinated while in office. **William McKinley and James A. Garfield**

We both have the same first name. **William McKinley and William (Bill) Clinton**

66

| | | | |
|---|---|---|---|
| Herbert C. Hoover | James (Jimmy) E. Carter, Jr. | Martin Van Buren | Theodore Roosevelt |

Name the presidents pictured above that match these statements. You may need to research some of the statements to write the name of the correct president.

We were both born in New York. **Martin Van Buren and Theodore Roosevelt**

The two of us served as governors of states. **Jimmy Carter and Theodore Roosevelt**

We both served as vice president. **Martin Van Buren and Theodore Roosevelt**

The three of us were in office during times of economic trouble. **Martin Van Buren, Herbert C. Hoover, and Jimmy Carter**

The three of us served only one term each. **Martin Van Buren, Herbert C. Hoover, and Jimmy Carter**

We were both elected as Republicans. **Theodore Roosevelt and Herbert C. Hoover**

We were both elected as Democrats. **Martin Van Buren and Jimmy Carter**

67

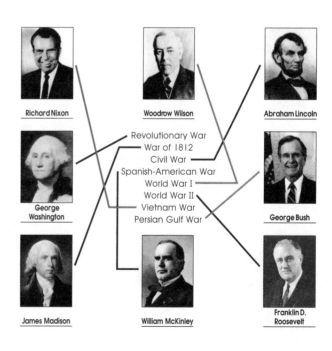

68

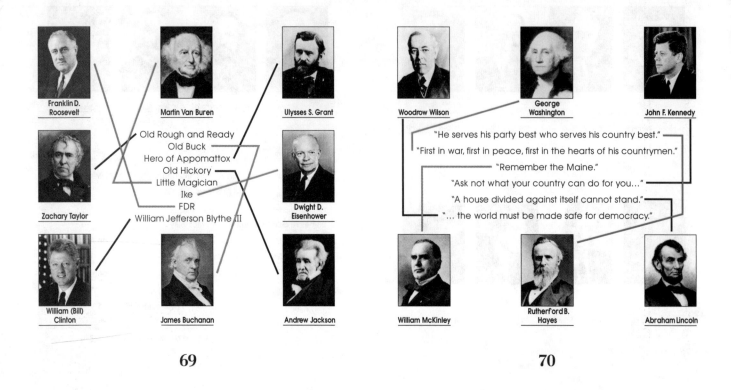

**69**

Franklin D. Roosevelt

Martin Van Buren

Ulysses S. Grant

Old Rough and Ready
Old Buck
Hero of Appomattox
Old Hickory
Little Magician
Ike
FDR
William Jefferson Blythe III

Zachary Taylor

Dwight D. Eisenhower

William (Bill) Clinton

James Buchanan

Andrew Jackson

**70**

Woodrow Wilson

George Washington

John F. Kennedy

"He serves his party best who serves his country best."
"First in war, first in peace, first in the hearts of his countrymen."
"Remember the Maine."
"Ask not what your country can do for you…"
"A house divided against itself cannot stand."
"… the world must be made safe for democracy."

William McKinley

Rutherford B. Hayes

Abraham Lincoln

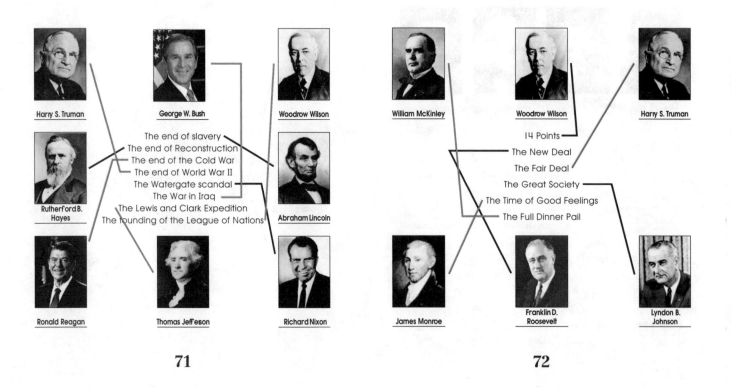

**71**

Harry S. Truman

George W. Bush

Woodrow Wilson

The end of slavery
The end of Reconstruction
The end of the Cold War
The end of World War II
The Watergate scandal
The War in Iraq
The Lewis and Clark Expedition
The founding of the League of Nations

Rutherford B. Hayes

Abraham Lincoln

Ronald Reagan

Thomas Jefferson

Richard Nixon

**72**

William McKinley

Woodrow Wilson

Harry S. Truman

14 Points
The New Deal
The Fair Deal
The Great Society
The Time of Good Feelings
The Full Dinner Pail

James Monroe

Franklin D. Roosevelt

Lyndon B. Johnson